Coven In Times Past

By the same author:

Tales from Four Towns
Death, Destruction, Crime and Notable News from 19th Century
Walsall, Wednesbury, West Bromwich and Wolverhampton

Coven In Times Past

Paul Robinson

Penk Publishing

Copyright © 2015 by Paul Robinson
All rights reserved. This book or any portion thereof may not be reproduced or used in any manner whatsoever without the express written permission of the publisher.

Paul Robinson has asserted his right under the Copyright, Designs and Patents Act, 1988, to be identified as the author of this work.

ISBN 978-1-326-12160-0

Penk Publishing

email: penk.publishing@gmail.com

To Alex, Lewis & Elysia

Contents

List of Illustrations 9
Preface 13
Acknowledgements 15
Introduction 17
Chapter 1 - Buildings 21
Chapter 2 - Mills and Farms 67
Chapter 3 - Road, Rail and Water 103
Chapter 4 - People, Occupations and Pastimes . . . 155
Chapter 5 - Making the News 185
Chapter 6 - Public Houses 215
Appendix 1 243
Appendix 2 245
Endnotes 246

List of Illustrations

1	Advertisement for school 1834	23
2	School Lane c1840	24
3	The old school	25
4	The old school, 1980s	25
5	Old school gardens	26
6	Vicars of Coven	27
7	St Paul's church	28
8	St Paul's church	29
9	Benchmark on St Paul's church	30
10	The Methodist chapel	31
11	Methodist Sunday School	31
12	Coven Heath chapel	32
13	The first Memorial Hall	33
14	Wiggin's Stores	34
15	Coven Stores	35
16	James Preston and Frank Till	36
17	The Village Foundry	38
18	The Village Foundry c.1960	38
19	Coven House	39
20	Coven House	40
21	Coven House shop	40
22	The Homage	42
23	Shops at Coven	42
24	Cottage near The Homage	43
25	Brewood Road seen from New Homage	44
26	Cottages near Harben Works	45

27	The Beeches	46
28	The Croft	48
29	Oaklands Cottage	48
30	Brewood Road cottages	49
31	Brewood Road cottages	50
32	Cottage at Cross Green	51
33	Forge Cottage	53
34	Forge Pool	54
35	Recreation ground	55
36	Old Heath House	56
37	Pool near Clewley	58
38	Brook Cottage	59
39	The Rookery, Standeford	60
40	The Woodlands	61
41	Standeford Lodge	62
42	Cottage at Standeford	63
43	Wayside Cottage	64
44	Darelyn Caravan Park	65
45	Standeford Mill pond	71
46	Coven Farm c.1930	72
47	Coven Farm	74
48	Coven Farm pigsties	74
49	Near Coven Farm	75
50	Three Hammers Farm	76
51	Three Hammers Farm cottages	77
52	Grange Farm	78
53	Grange Farm circa 1940	78
54	Lawn Farm	80
55	Poplars Farm Fields	81
56	The old War Memorial	82
57	Site of War Memorial	82
58	Manor Farm	84
59	Manor Farm	84
60	Derelict buildings at Manor Farm	85
61	Paradise Farm	85
62	Paradise Lane	86

63	Aspley Farm	88
64	Antler found at Brewood Park Farm	90
65	Brewood Park Farm, house circa 1938.	90
66	Frederick J Keeling	91
67	Brewood Park Farm 1918	93
68	Brewood Park Farm, 1946.	94
69	Brewood Park Farm cottages	95
70	Foomer fields	97
71	Advertisement for railway construction	106
72	Early Grand Junction train	106
73	Slade Heath railway bridge	110
74	Station Drive, Four Ashes	115
75	Proposed railway to Brewood	117
76	ROF Featherstone	119
77	ROF Featherstone detail	120
78	Roads at Slade Heath	121
79	Old lane to Crateford	122
80	Poplars Farm	123
81	Old lane at Standeford	124
82	Paths at Coven Heath	125
83	Traction engine at Slade Heath	126
84	The A449 dual carriageway	127
85	Road at The Harrows	128
86	Waterworks construction	129
87	Waterworks boiler being delivered	130
88	Boilers at the waterworks	130
89	Slade Heath Pumping Station	131
90	Waterworks steam engine	131
91	Building and boring debris	132
92	Hordern Cottages	137
93	Ball Lane canal bridge	137
94	Cross Green canal bridge	138
95	Bridge at Slade Heath	140
96	Slade Heath benchmark	140
97	Waterworks canal wharf	141
98	Stafford Road bridge, Brinsford	142

99	Avenue Bridge	143
100	Bridge at Lower Pendeford	144
101	The Penk around Coven	146
102	River Penk at The Bront, 1875	147
103	Bridge at Brewood Park Farm	148
104	Marks on Jackson's Bridge	149
105	Benchmark, Jackson's Bridge	149
106	'Sandyford Brook'	150
107	Standeford bridge	153
108	Pinfold Croft	158
109	The Gardens of England	168
110	An Aveling steam plough	171
111	The Village Foundry	172
112	John Smith maker's plate	172
113	John Smith's '122' locomotive	173
114	John Smith's 'Ajax'	174
115	The locomotive 'Grosvenor'	176
116	Theatre programs	180
117	The Ball Inn	220
118	The Golden Ball in the 1950s	221
119	The Rainbow Inn around 1910	226
120	The Rainbow after the Great War	226
121	David Kirk & Joseph Ward Jugs	230
122	Samuel Martin Kirk	232
123	Four Ashes Farm, 1900	233
124	Albrighton Hunt at Four Ashes	233
125	The Four Ashes, 1926	234
126	Coach advertisement	234
127	Four Ashes Inn	235
128	The Harrows, 1926	238
129	The Harrows bowling green	238
130	The Anchor Inn, 1907	240
131	The Anchor Inn, circa 1935	242
132	The Anchor Inn, circa 1955	242

Preface

One of the biggest challenges when writing this book was deciding where to 'pitch' the content. Local history books often fall into two camps; scholarly works that contain all the facts and references but are not exactly 'page-turners', and historical 'photo albums' containing captioned pictures but little else. To many people, local history is synonymous with events in their childhood or in their grandparent's era, whereas for others it may mean delving into the very earliest history of a locality. I hope this work falls somewhere between all of these extremes by going far enough into Coven's past to make it interesting while containing over a hundred photographs and diagrams.

There may be mistakes in this book, it does, after all, contain a lot of names and even more dates, but anyone using it as a basis for further research can check the facts for themselves using the sources listed near the end. Where a little speculation has crept in, I have made it plain that this is what it is. It will also be seen that some buildings, features or people seem to be glossed over or even omitted altogether and this is simply because I have been unable to find out anything about them that would interest the average reader, not that they have been purposely ignored or forgotten.

Acknowledgements

As someone who has lived in Coven for a mere 20 years I have relied upon people who have lived here for much longer to provide information and to put me right whenever I 'got the wrong end of the stick', something that is all to easy to do when looking into the past. Credit is due to the following individuals and organisations for helping with my research and contributing information and photographs:

> The compilers of two photographic albums of Coven, Suzanne Proudley and Frank Lowe, and the generous contributors to those albums:

> A Merrick, D Sargent, V Adams, J Barnes, C Bailey, T Berry, T Banks, M Bickford, D Bickford, S Blount, J Bradbury, L Bradbury, S Brindley, S Caton, R Dampier, G Edwards, J Ellick, E Evans, M Fellows, R Frost, V Francis, M Groves, L Hammond, Harben Engineering, G Lanchbury, J Lowe, M Heath, E Merrick, D Morris, D Newcombe, W Painter, G Peake, D Piper, R Price, B Powell, R Proudley, S Proudley, W Proudley, R Richards, E Shenton, C Shipley, L Simms, B Taylor, A Till, L Wiles, T Williams, C Wood, P Williams, J Wright, H Dodd, A Nicholls, J Hooson.

> The staff at Stafford Record Office, Wolverhampton Archives and the William Salt Library.

Chris Pattison - South Staffs Water Archives, Kevin Arnold - The Village News, Maggie O'Brien - Brewood & Coven Parish Council, Leo Whitlock - Kentish Gazette, Michael Christensen OBE, Linda Dutton, Marie Nicholls, Kathryn Robinson, Mark Robinson, Pam Clay, David Kirk, Mary Parton, Ray Shill, Alex Appleton Collection, Wendy Kirk, Sue Piper, Clive Richards, Nora M Kirk

...and the numerous residents of the village and surrounding hamlets, who never gave me their names but gave freely of their time and encouragement.

I have asked permission to reproduce photographs where the owner of the original is known, but some photographs from the previously mentioned albums are of unknown origin or were taken by individuals who are now deceased. If you are the originator of any such photograph I trust that you will sanction its use after the event in the interest of illustrating the history of Coven. I would like to have included a few other photographs and maps that are held in the various Staffordshire Archives but their reproduction fees made this infeasible. Places where additional photographs, documents and maps may be found are mentioned in the text.

Introduction

Although the historical features of Coven and its immediate vicinity have been included in a few other books dealing with Brewood, this book is a little different in that it tries to flesh out the history of the area with stories about people and the environment in which they lived and worked. It therefore falls somewhere between the usual and somewhat arbitrary classifications of 'local' and 'social' history.

Where available, descriptions of places or events are included in the written or spoken words of those that saw them at first hand, in order to give a better feel for the era concerned. Some of these quotations contain punctuation, capitalisation and spelling that aren't used today but I have copied them verbatim.

The widespread distribution of newspapers and publishing of local directories, followed by the start of countrywide census-taking and the advent of photography, allows us to examine the affairs of ordinary people from the late eighteenth century onwards, in greater detail than in any previous era. This period then, from the end of the 1700s up until the first quarter of the twentieth century, is the main focus of 'Coven in Times Past'. The region covered is approximately from Paradise to Somerford in an east-to-west span and from Four Ashes down to Coven Heath in the opposite compass.

Before getting into detail about the more recent past, it is worth very briefly reviewing what is known about the history of the area in general up until the end of the 18th century. At one time there were two Bronze Age 'round barrows' lying between the present-day Fours Ashes industrial estate and Saredon Brook, although they were ploughed-out many years ago. These simple burial mounds could have been constructed at any time between about 2,500 BC and the start of the Iron Age, around 700 BC. Whichever point in this date range they were from, they constituted the earliest archaeology in this area.

The next direct evidence comes from the era of Roman occupation, 55 BC until about 450 AD, during which the military camp at Pennocrucium, Engleton Villa and Watling Street, all some way north of Coven, came into being. An object found at The Laches in the 1600s was thought to be the brass head of a Roman catapult bolt but the contemporary illustration in Robert Plot's 'Natural History Of Staffordshire', shows that it was actually a Bronze Age socketed axe-head and therefore considerably older. A similar artefact was unearthed more recently near Shaw Hall Farm.

In the early Medieval period, sometimes called the Anglo Saxon period or the 'Dark Ages', Brinsford and Standeford are mentioned in a 'Boundary Clause' - a document detailing the extent of particular land ownership. Surprisingly, some of the features mentioned in this ninth century schedule are still obvious today - Standeford for example is referred to as the place of the 'stoney ford'. It is around this time that the name of Coven is thought to have come into use. The name is believed to derive from the Anglo Saxon word 'cofum' meaning 'the place at the huts' or 'the place at the cove', a 'cove' having the same meaning as today, ie a sheltered location.

In the Domesday survey, completed in 1086, Coven is described as a very small village of just eight households, with arable land for two plough teams, about three acres of meadow and a substantial acreage of woodland (it was after all at the margins of Cannock Chase at the time). Before the Conquest, the manor of Coven was held by 'Alric' but it was under Norman control, in the hands of Robert of Stafford, during William's reign.

Over the succeeding centuries, and especially from the latter part of the 15th century, when regulation spread into almost every aspect of peoples lives, the number of documentary sources increases substantially. Many of these records have yet to be examined in detail, and no doubt some will contain interesting information about

Coven, although the majority will most likely cover rather dry financial and legal matters. Court records from this period might be of more interest as they are likely to reveal greater detail about individuals and their activities.

In 1651, after escaping the Battle of Worcester and hiding at Boscobel, Charles II is known to have passed through Pendeford and Coven Heath on his epic journey into temporary exile. Mr Huntbache, who occupied a large house at Brinsford, provided shelter to Lord Wilmot after the same conflict.

A couple of decades after the Civil War, Coven itself had about 40 houses and perhaps therefore, 150 inhabitants. At this time, iron-working was carried out in the area immediately north and west of the village where it persisted until the 19th century.

William Yates recorded three water-driven mills in this area on his 1775 map, one at Coven Heath, one near Pendeford Hall and another just off Coven Lawn, although each could have been in existence for centuries beforehand. The mill at Coven Lawn seems to have fallen out of use at some time before the 1830s.

During the nineteenth century, lock-making and a small scale engineering industry developed in the area but these disappeared as manufacturing and mass production became concentrated in the Black Country, Birmingham and Wolverhampton. A few small industrial concerns continued in the village through the twentieth century, but industry and commerce in the nearby towns became the principal employers alongside local agriculture.

Towards the end of the twentieth century, various new housing developments came into being, transforming Coven into a typical modern 'commuter belt' village, with the vast majority of residents now employed far beyond the houses, workshops, streets and fields of Coven in times past.

Chapter 1
Buildings

Although no building in Coven is more than 450 years old, it is quite probable that some occupy the sites of earlier structures. We know that Coven was inhabited at the time of Domesday, compiled 20 years after the Norman Conquest of 1066, and these medieval folk must have dwelt somewhere. The peasantry who worked the land in that distant era would have lived in crude wooden-framed houses, possibly with wattle-and-daub walls and thatched roofs. The local knight, on the next rung of the feudal system, would no doubt have lived in a superior dwelling and then, as now, it would make sense to re-use an existing site if it offered a convenient water supply, suitable land to eke out an existence and a measure of security.

In addition to reusing sites, many of the buildings in Coven have themselves had various uses at different times and, where known, these are noted in the descriptions. For example, some of the buildings in this chapter are known to have served as farmhouses in the past but are included here, rather than in the following chapter, as they now have entirely residential use or are no longer in a farmland setting.

Public Buildings

The School & School House

John Hughes ran a private 'day school' in Coven as early as 1832 and it seems likely that this school building was used for worship before St Paul's church came into being. Around 1840 John Williams was listed in the tithe apportionments as occupying a house with garden and school on the corner of Light Ash Lane, but curiously, no building is shown in that plot on the associated map - the same plot is also listed as arable land known as 'Intake'. There was a house directly opposite the site, beside the brook, so perhaps this was the original location of the school.

Plans for what is now the 'old school' and schoolmaster's house, were drawn up by Edward Banks in July 1858, around the time that St Paul's became a National School. This building originally had a very church-like entrance, with a small bell tower and three gothic-style windows above the porch - these were later bricked-up but traces can still be seen on the frontage. It was extended and altered at back and front as more capacity was required, but when it could no longer hold the requisite number of pupils, a completely new school was built beside it.

Children were separated into three groups in the old school; infants in the smaller (eastern) part, and boys and girls each having about half of the main building. The playground at the front of the building was for boys, the girls playground being separated by walls from the boys on one side and the schoolhouse garden on the other.

In 1871 Joseph Hand Jackson was the schoolmaster, followed in 1881 by Edward Hodges, assisted by his siblings.

John Handel Hall was headmaster from the beginning of the twentieth century until at least 1911. John and his wife May, who was also a teacher, married at Birmingham in 1898 and moved to Coven shortly afterwards. Mr Hall had attended the Church of England teacher training college at Saltley, Birmingham and was able to stand-in if the local vicar was indisposed.

In those days, many pupils had to walk a considerable distance

TERMS of MR. HUGHES'S COMMERCIAL, MATHEMATICAL and CLASSICAL ACADEMY, COVEN, NEAR BREWOOD.

	£.	S.	D.	
Board and Tuition in Reading, Writing (plain & ornamental), Arithmetic, English Grammar, Elocution, Short Hand, Geography, the Use of the Globes, and Mathematics in general,	22	0	0	per Ann.
Pupils under ten years	20	0	0	Do.
Latin, Greek, and French, each extra,	1	10	0	Do.
Washing	2	0	0	Do.

Mr. H. informs those Parents and Guardians who may honour him with their patronage, that he will endeavour to facilitate the progress of those Pupils committed to his care, in the various departments of commercial, mathematical, and classical Literature.

Mr. H. confidently asserts that no Academy possesses superior means for the acquisition of knowledge: his plans of Tuition have received general approbation, and have been found by repeated experiments to be attended with unusual success; that those Pupils committed to his care will be enabled to discharge their stations in life, either professional or commercial, with honour to themselves, and credit to their Instructors.

The School is situated in the pleasant and healthy village of Coven, two miles from Brewood, and five from Wolverhampton.

Books, Maps, Charts, Manuscripts, &c. always at hand, for the Scholars' use.

The School will be re-opened on Monday, 16th July, 1832.

Private Tuition in any of the above branches of learning.

Figure 1: Advertisement for the school in 1834.

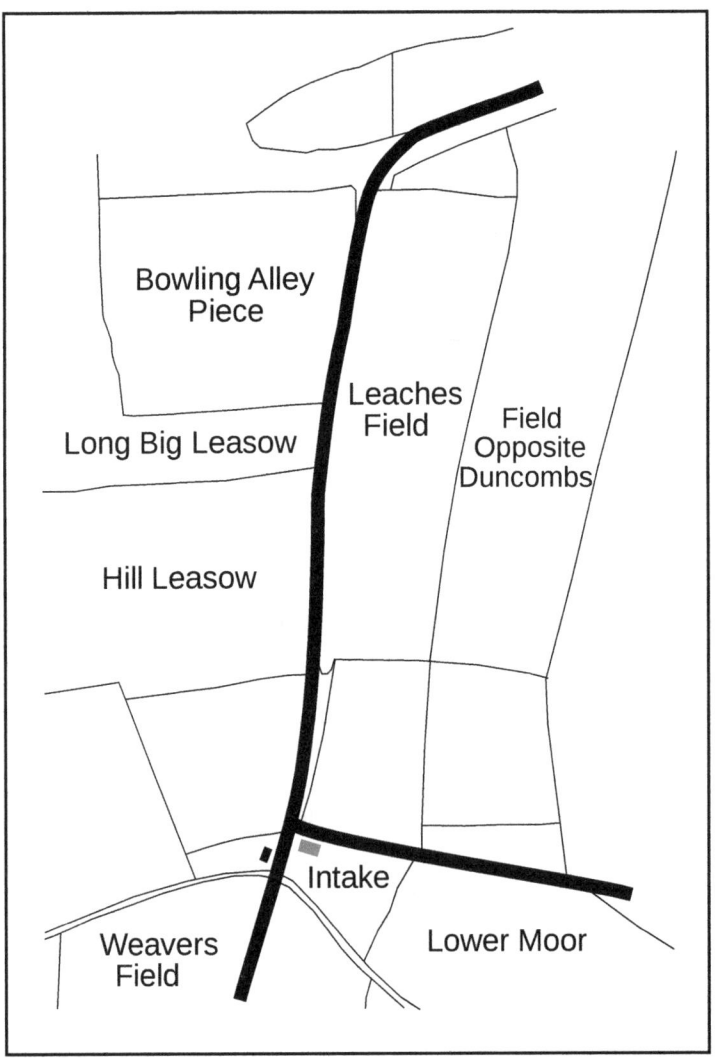

Figure 2: Fields along school lane around 1840. The house beside the brook may have been the location of the first school in Coven - the present day 'old school' is shown opposite, in the field known as 'Intake'.

Figure 3: A view of the school along Light Ash rather than School Lane as the postcard suggests. (L. Dutton)

Figure 4: The old school was extended as increases in capacity were required. The eastern third was completely demolished during recent refurbishment. (M. Nicholls)

Figure 5: Part of the school gardens in 1937.

to and from the various farms scattered around the area as there was no public transport; some children came from as far as Bilbrook, regardless of the weather.

The school had its own gardens, on the land now occupied by Broad Acres, where children were allocated their own plots to grow flowers and vegetables. The recreation ground, which occupied most of the corner between School Lane and Brewood Road, was used for school sports and was home turf for the local football team. This land, constrained by the brook and the angle of these two roads was known as 'Weavers Field' in the early 1800s. The large sloping field on the opposite corner, through which the school footpath runs, was known as 'Broomfield'.

In the late 1950s the landowner wanted to build housing on the site, but permission was only forthcoming for the Greenacres estate once land further along School Lane had been secured for a new recreation ground. The present-day children's play-park and part of the new playing fields lie on what was once known as 'Leaches Field'.

Plans for the outdoor recreation centre (or 'holiday camp' as it was called at the time) at The Laches were submitted by Willenhall

Figure 6: Three Coven vicars and their periods of tenure: G Roper 1899-1902, R B Forrester 1902-1915, H Edwards 1915-1937.

Urban Council as far back as 1932.[1]

St Paul's Church

St Paul's was built on a field known as 'Upper Cow Pasture', using locally quarried stone, and was consecrated in 1857. Inglis Monckton was the first vicar and remained in the post almost until the end of the century, having served an incredible 41 years by the time he died in 1899. He was rather eccentric, objecting to members of his congregation wearing buttonholes and insisting that women's hats should be very plain. He was not averse to taking fancy hats from the heads of women and offering them a straw boater instead! It was said that he also attempted to prove everything in the bible by means of strange numerical calculations. In 1876, J Douglas Gawn was appointed as the Reverend Monckton's assistant and George Rowlands, who lived at Standeford Lodge, took up the curacy in 1891.

Reverend Roper suffered ill-health during his tenure due to tuberculosis and John Hall from the school frequently took services in his stead. Mr Hall also had to stand in for Reverend Forrester on occasion, as this clergyman was afflicted by epilepsy. Mr Forrester sometimes suffered partial seizures, during which he would try to remove his clothes. Sometimes this happened when he was out walking and, on more than one occasion, when he was taking

Figure 7: St Paul's around the time of the Second World War. (M. Nicholls)

a service, at which point Mr Hall would usher him into the vestry and take his place.

Before the Memorial Hall was built, a corrugated metal structure which stood beside the church, served as the village hall. Known as the 'Iron Room', it lay where the new vicarage now stands. It was used as a soup kitchen after the Great War and was later used by the WI, the mothers' union, the Sunday School and for many social gatherings. The building was destroyed by fire in the 1950s, probably as a result of arson, but its demise spurred the campaign for a new hall, more suited to the expanding village.

There is an Ordnance Survey benchmark on St Paul's church - it is one of the so called 'Flush Bracket' type. These are uniquely numbered metallic plates cemented in place, rather than being a simple mark cut in to the stonework.

The garden of the old vicarage, on the east side of the church, was the venue for an annual garden party and other outdoor events.[2]

Figure 8: A postcard view of the church in the early years of the twentieth century. (L. Dutton)

Figure 9: 'Flush bracket' type benchmark (inset) on St Paul's church. (Author)

Methodist Chapel & Sunday School

A date-stone on Coven Methodist Chapel declares that it was erected in 1839 but services had been held at John Smith's adjacent premises for at least ten years before this date. The chapel was opened in September by Reverend Macdonald of Birmingham and a collection at the opening service raised fifty one pounds. When added to the £120 raised beforehand, this cleared almost all of the debt outstanding on the property from day one.

In 1909 Joseph Cooper of Coven, conducted two special services at Cannock Wood Methodist Chapel to mark the anniversary of the Sunday School there. A group of children specially trained by Miss Keeling (presumably one of those from Brewood Park) sang and gave recitals.

Coven's own Methodist Sunday School opened in January 1925 at a cost of £1,300. Commonly known as the 'Methodist Hall', it was used among other things as a venue for local Girl Guides

Figure 10: Coven Methodist Chapel in 2014. (Author)

Figure 11: The Methodist Sunday School building in 2010. (Author)

meetings. It stood on the opposite side of Lawn Lane to the chapel, near the junction with Brewood Road. The space in front was used as a public car park for the adjacent shops, until the building was demolished towards the end of 2011, after which, houses were built on the entire site.[3]

Coven Heath Chapel

Figure 12: Coven Heath Chapel around 1950. (L. Dutton)

Theodosia Hinckes, "a lady of considerable fortune", sponsored the building of various churches and schools in Bushbury parish, including the minuscule chapel on Coven Heath. Born in London in 1792, but descended from a wealthy Wolverhampton family, she remained a spinster and had a close association with the church throughout her life. She lived at the family home in Tettenhall Wood and was great friends with Rebecca Moore, wife of the Archdeacon of Stafford. The Moores lived in Cathedral Close beside Lichfield Cathedral, which was where Miss Hinckes spent her last days, passing away in 1874 at the age of 81. A portrait of Theodosia Hinckes in her younger years can be seen at the cathedral.[4]

The Memorial Hall

The destruction of the 'iron room' beside the church added impetus to the campaign for a new village hall and a site on the recreation ground was earmarked in the mid 1950s. When sufficient funds had been raised, work on the new hall could begin and the former officers' mess at Wheaton Aston's wartime aerodrome was purchased, disassembled and re-erected in Coven with a new brick frontage.

This building lasted some twenty years before being adjudged too small and somewhat unsafe. Fund-raising began once more and the new hall was finally opened in 1975. It was built beside its predecessor, which was eventually pulled down to provide a larger car park.

Figure 13: The first Memorial Hall soon after opening. (M. Nicholls)

The Telephone Exchange

This was originally located on the east side of the Stafford Road between Standeford and Four Ashes. It was moved into Coven village around 1970 but is still known as Standeford Exchange.

Shops & Workshops

Wiggin's Stores

This building was owned and occupied by Thomas Wade around 1840, before becoming the 'New Inn' about twenty years later. Mr Wade farmed several fields at the rear of the property that now lie beneath Darelyn caravan park. By the end of the century it had become a bakery and grocer's shop run by Henry and Ann Wiggin (although the business name was 'E A Wiggin'). Their son, Thomas George, was still in the area a decade later; he was a hay and straw dealer living at Meadow House, Coven Heath.

Figure 14: Village baker James Preston and his family at Wiggins Stores, 1906. (Author's collection)

The baker from around 1906 was James Preston, assisted by Arthur Bowen, Frank Till and later Vic Francis. Flour was brought by cart from Four Ashes station and the bread was baked in ovens situated in outbuildings at the rear of the property. Deliveries were made on foot, by bicycle, by horse-drawn cart and later by motorised van. Winifred Wasall, whose father farmed at Mount Pleas-

Figure 15: The shop in the 1970s.

ant in the 1930s, worked as a housemaid for Mr Preston.

James Preston was originally a train driver but had lost his leg in an accident. He and his wife adopted Victor Francis after the First World War - the young Francis and his father had fled their native Belgium during the war and been billeted at the Beeches.

Mr Till began the Darelyn caravan park in a field at the rear of the property at some point in the 1950s and lived in the bungalow at the front of the site, although he later moved to a house on Brewood Road near the Anchor. He was a local councillor and was instrumental in raising money for the village hall. He was also a champion breeder of curly-coated retrievers - the Darelyn name (pronounced 'dare lin') being his Kennel Club prefix. A Philip Till, who may have been one of Frank Till's ancestors, owned a cottage and gardens at Light Ash in 1824 as did one Joshua Brown. This was the exception rather than the rule as most of the land around Coven at this time was in the hands of Messrs Monckton, Smith, Bickford, Shenstone and Richards.

Figure 16: Mr Preston, the baker, and his assistant Frank Till, in the garden of the bakery, with the Homage in the background. (M.Nicholls)

The shop traded under various names during the twentieth century and Mr Francis went on to run Coven Stores, as it later became, until his retirement in the 1980s. The property today has residential use but, with the exception of the bay windows and stopping-up of doorways, is little changed externally from its original form.

The Village Foundry

This imposing works stood at the very top of Lawn Lane on the eastern side. Built in the 1850s, the foundry had various uses over its 130-year history. After being used as Smith's works, it became a brewery, run by Frederick and Henry Charles Coleclough around 1900, and in the middle of the twentieth century was occupied by John McLean & Sons, the house-builders who became part of Tarmac in the 1970s. It was finally used by the 'Go Plant' company, a subsidiary of Tarmac, before demolition around 1989.

The foundry and the Methodist chapel were built on land either side of the Smith family home, a cottage dating back to the 1500s. This timber-framed structure, which had been mostly rebuilt in brick, was used as a doctor's surgery during the 1960s but was pulled down at the same time as the works. Land opposite the cottage was used as an orchard, the housing development known as 'Orchard Close' standing on the site today.

A house known as 'Greystones Cottage' neighboured the foundry on the Brewood Road; it was replaced by modern housing in the first decade of this millennium.

Coven House

Coven House, a substantial dwelling built around 1800, stood on higher ground opposite the top of Lawn Lane. Around 1840 the building was owned by Mr Shenstone of Standeford Mill but occupied by widow Dorothy Hughes who, with her sons, farmed nearby fields and ran a butchers shop.

In 1871 James Hughes, a farmer and butcher lived at Coven House and in 1881 George Smith and his wife ran a grocery store

Figure 17: Preston's bakery delivery van passing the foundry.

Figure 18: The village foundry around 1960. (M.Nicholls)

Figure 19: Piper's nursery with The Homage at right. Trees bordering 'The Bront' form the backdrop to the village from this angle. (S. Piper)

there as well as farming over 30 acres in the village. There was also a grocery shop at Slade Heath at this time.

The house was occupied from 1947 by Cyril Piper and his family, the grounds being used for their market garden and nursery business. Produce was sold at Wolverhampton and Dudley markets and from the shop on the right-hand side of the property. The house was demolished in the 1960s and the business moved to Watling Street, near Gailey. Housing stands on the Coven House site today but its past lives on in the name of 'The Nurseries'.

The Homage

This building is said to be one of the earliest all-brick houses in the county of Staffordshire. Although it has probably been a residence for most of its life, it has had many other uses during the last 150 years. The house was built during the reign of Charles II, its prominent date-stone reading 'WM 1679'.

It seems very likely that it was first owned by William Mansell,

Figure 20: Coven House in the 1950s. (S. Piper)

Figure 21: Coven House shop, with an advert for 'Lyons Tea' in the window. (M. Nicholls)

who had lived in Coven since at least 1668 and was in charge of the local iron furnace and two forges, all of which belonged to ironmaster Philip Foley.

Henry Richards, a local 'yeoman', drew up his will in 1669 and amongst his possessions, he listed two parcels of land known as 'the homages'. Mr Richards died in, or shortly before, December 1672 and pursuant to his will, an inventory of his goods and chattels was drawn up. One of the three 'appraisers' or valuers of this inventory was William Mansell.

In 1725 a William Mansell, 'husbandman of Coven' was thrown into debtors prison; whether it was the aforementioned Mansell, who would by this time be an old man, or perhaps his son, is not known.

Mansell's son, Thomas, married Eleanor Pitchford in 1685 and their pre-nuptial agreement contains a wealth of detail about properties in Coven. Unfortunately none of the buildings mentioned can be identified (or have survived) and many of the fields named in the document have disappeared under housing developments. There are a number of Mansell burials at St Mary & St Chad, Brewood for the period 1659 to 1836, including William, his wife Marabella, Thomas and other descendants.

At one time The Homage was the home for priests from Brewood. In 1861 William Piggott was the 'receiver' at the Post Office located here. It remained a Post Office until at least 1904 and at this time there were wall-mounted letter boxes at Standeford and Cross Green, which were emptied just before seven each evening.

It served as Coven Police Station in the early part of the twentieth century - William John Barrett being stationed there in the years before the Great War - and also housed a draper's shop run by Mrs Nickolds, whose husband Henry was the postman.

In 1834, Joseph Lloyd and Catherine Williams were shop-keepers in Coven. There was a shop on the Brewood Road opposite the bridge carrying the path to Brewood Park Farm and Walter Hollis ran another shop nearby in 1841, possibly at Brook House. At the same time, Leonard Reynolds ran his shoemaker's shop from the cottages belonging to Grange Farm and James Roberts had a shop

Figure 22: Early 1900s view of The Homage with a carriage departing at left and two ladies in front of Wiggin's Stores. The extension on the right of the building served as a shop.

Figure 23: View from the road in front of the Homage in the mid-20th century, showing the Post Office and butcher's shop.

Figure 24: This cottage stood immediately opposite The Homage (just off picture to the right), until the 1970s.

at his house at the bottom of Cinder Hill near Brewood Road.

About this time, Samuel and Thomas Shotton ran a shop on Lawn Lane and John Hadley had one opposite Standeford Mill. It seems that Messrs Lloyd and Samuel Shotton were not full-time shopkeepers as at the 1841 census their occupations were given as 'locksmith' and 'agricultural labourer' respectively.

By 1851 there were three shop-keepers in the village and shoemakers at Light Ash and Standeford; there was also a cobbler's shop near the Rainbow Inn during later years.

A view taken across the front garden of the Homage looking towards Grange Farm was probably taken from a bedroom of 'New Homage Cottages'. A very similar photograph of around 1920 was taken by Arthur Whatton (see below), suggesting that this is where he now lived, his former shop at The Rookery having become a Post Office. The building right of centre was known as 'Ivy Cottage' at the turn of the century and has been replaced by the present-day 'Green Ivy House'.

There was a building on the site of New Homage Cottages a

Figure 25: View across the front garden of The Homage, circa 1920. (M. Nicholls)

hundred years before the present structure was built. Edwards' coal merchants and haulage contractors began their business from a house near the Anchor Inn but moved their yard to the rear of these cottages in 1932. Houses have since been built on the site. Edwards' obtained their coal from a colliery at Cheslyn Hay, whereas earlier coal-merchants brought it from Littleton by cart. Coal has also been delivered to the village via the pathway from the canal at Slade Heath.[5]

Houses, Cottages & Caravans

School Lane Cottages

These cottages stood at Standeford Green, the Harrows end of School Lane, until the mid-1970s when the adjacent Harben works were extended. The extension almost completely enclosed the dwellings before they were demolished.

The cottage almost opposite, which was recently refurbished,

Figure 26: Cottages near the Harben works in the 1970s. (H.N. Harben)

was presumably occupied by the Duncomb family before the start of the nineteenth century, as the field across the road was known as 'Field Opposite Duncombs'! The Duncomb surname can be found in records relating to Coven going back to the 1600s.

The Beeches

This late Georgian house was owned and occupied in the 1830s by Henry Richards, who also owned the adjacent Poplars farmhouse. The plot occupied by The Beeches once extended alongside Brewood Road as far as School Lane and included sunken gardens, and, in later years, a swimming pool near to the house. Around 1840, the land beyond the immediate garden was a meadow which was, in name at least, in the tenure of John Smith junior who was then just about 10 years-old!

The East and West Beeches housing developments occupy the majority of the land today.

Beeches Lodge, a cottage standing at the front of the property,

Figure 27: Rear view of The Beeches in the late 1980s.

is believed to have been a coach house. The rear wall has traces of a large doorway to allow access from the yard.

For about three years either side of the First World War the house was inhabited by Mr Hughes and his family. Hughes was a chemist who had emigrated to Canada some years beforehand but returned in order that his children should receive a British education.

The Croft

In 1802, four properties and a number of parcels of land in Coven, belonging to the late Henry Sherrett (probably the same gentleman who served as a churchwarden at Brewood during the 1770s) were put up for auction. One of these, probably The Croft, is described as "a modern and well built messauge or dwelling house, in complete repair, with the Barn, Stable, convenient Outbuildings, Yard and Garden". A tenant of one of the properties mentioned was William Till, another surname that crops up frequently in the history of the area.

The Croft was occupied by William Chambley in the 1840s and Joseph James, also a farmer, lived at the house opposite. This building, possibly known as 'Croft Cottage' or later as 'Church House', stood on the corner almost opposite the Croft until the middle of the twentieth century, members of the Hartshorn family living there from at least 1911.

There was a sizeable pond behind outbuildings at the back of The Croft in the 1830s and on the western side, beside the road, was an orchard and a rickyard. The house was extended at the rear some time before 1880 and two decades later a Mrs Hughes was advertising apartments to let within the house on "moderate terms".

In 1911, Edward Jackson and his sons, who had recently moved here from Dorset, lived at the Croft and operated the adjacent farm, part of which was where the Croft Garage now stands - in later years it was a poultry farm. The property was put up for sale in 1924 and around this time, Thomas Bryan lived at the aforementioned Croft Cottage.[6]

Oaklands Cottage

This house was built some time before 1824 and fields at the rear, which were later cut in two by the dual carriageway, were once owned by John Smith. In 1841 William Brown lived here and there were barns on the west side of the property where another house now stands. At that time, the field immediately behind the house was farmed by John Smith but owned by Henry Richards.

In the first decade of the twentieth century the Misses Higgs, spinsters in their forties, lived here. They operated an agricultural threshing business and were probably related to John Smith's business partner, John Higgs.

The cottage was later owned by the Bickford family and their depot was set up on land at the rear of the property. This was originally an agricultural engineering business formed by Frank Bickford but it later expanded to deal with heavy lorries. A caravan site also

Figure 28: A parade passing the Croft at the Silver Jubilee in 1977. (M.Nicholls)

Figure 29: The photograph was taken from the gateway at what was then the end of Church Lane.

Figure 30: Cottages and gardens at Brewood Road. (M. Nicholls)

occupied part of the site during the 1950s and 60s.

Brewood Road Cottages

The two rows of cottages either side of the road near the Rainbow Inn were built before 1840 and owned by John Smith. Those near Poplars Farm had allotment gardens behind a wall on the opposite side of the road. Some of the cottages had stairs at front and rear forming two separate dwellings and were home to some of Coven's lock-makers, with garden outbuildings serving as workshops.

When the cottages were demolished in the 1960s, a parade of shops with parking at front and rear were built on the gardens.

A view from the opposite end of this stretch of the Brewood Road shows the Rainbow and adjacent cottages, one of which housed a cobblers shop, and the old granary belonging to The Beeches. The buildings and pavement all appear in a dilapidated condition; demolition and re-building followed soon after this photograph was taken.

Figure 31: Cottages on Brewood Road seen from the opposite direction. (M. Nicholls)

In the early part of the twentieth century the local wheelwright was Bill Handley and although he lived in a cottage on the Brewood Road, his workshop was at Four Ashes - no doubt because of the Stafford Road traffic and the number of carriages and carts that took people and goods to and from the railway station.

A century beforehand, Jonathon Williams was the village wheelwright and Thomas Williams, possibly his son, followed the same profession in 1851, employing three individuals. Joseph Townsend at Slade Heath and Joseph Farmer at Coven Lawn carried on the same trade in the 1840s.[7]

Cross Green Cottage

The present-day 'Bluebell Cottage', standing on the south side of the canal bridge, is shown on Yates' map of 1775. In the early part of the nineteenth century there was a second cottage adjacent to this one, a little nearer the Anchor Inn, and set slightly further back

Figure 32: Bluebell Cottage around 1960, before the coming of the golf course and before it was extended.

from the road. Around 1840 Thomas Careless lived here and the field at the rear of the property, now the golf course, was known as 'Careless' Field'.

During Victoria's reign the cottage was used as a police station; located beside a main road, a canal and a public house, it was ideally situated to watch over these places that were sometimes subject to criminal activity. As well as keeping usual police records, stations such as this would keep a register of incidents that were not criminal in nature, such as breaches of by-laws, which could be passed to the local council for information or to enable civil action to be taken.

It served as a police station from at least 1861, when John Matthews was stationed there, and in 1901, constable Edward Beech lived there with his family.[8]

Stone House

This house stood on the east side of Somerford Lane at its junction with Brewood Road. It was said to have been regularly visited by Dr Samuel Johnson on his way to poetry readings at Somerford Hall. However, although the house is clearly marked on maps of 1834 and later, it is omitted from Yates' map of 1775. As Johnson died in 1784 it is still just possible that he visited the house.

In the late 1800s the building was known as Stone House Cottages and accommodated two separate families - whether it was originally a single dwelling is not known. A photograph of the building can be seen at Staffordshire Archives.

Sarah Fisher, a wealthy widow, moved here from Ombersley, Droitwich with her three adult children at some time before 1891. Twenty years later the house was inhabited by one of her sons, Crowther Smith Fisher, and her daughter, Florence Ellen. Mr Fisher, a retired mineral water manufacturer, had been in partnership with two other men during the 1880s, Herbert Perry and William Anderson, operating a mineral water and beer bottling business from premises at Dudley Street, Wolverhampton and at Birmingham. Mr Fisher may also have served as a parish councillor. He died in 1922 but his sister lived here alone until she passed away in 1935 when the house was sold. It was demolished at some time between 1940 and 1954.

There was a brickworks on the opposite side of the lane until the mid-1950s and the other side of the Brewood Road was also quarried. Known as Stradsfield Quarry, these pits had been worked from the early decades of the nineteenth century or beforehand. The stone they produced was used in the construction of several local buildings including St Paul's church and the churches at Bishops Wood and Lapley. Stone for a building on Brewood Park Farm may also have come from here although there is also a 'Quarry Field' within the farm. A building known as Stradsfield House stands upon the site today but workings to the rear of the property and on the opposite side of Brewood Road are still clearly visible.

In the nineteenth century, a remarkable series of dinosaur foot-

Figure 33: The cottage, with water pump before the front door, in 1917. (M. Nicholls)

prints were discovered in a quarry beside the road, about 200 yards from Stone House in the direction of Somerford. The bed of rock was said to be about 12 feet below the surface and was covered with a great number of prints from two species; Labyrinthodon, a squat crocodile-like creature with prints around ten inches long, and Rhynchosaurus, a beaked lizard, whose prints were under two inches.[9]

Forge Cottage

This house was constructed in the early 1700s, the forge opposite being in operation from the mid-17th century or earlier. Various maps of the early 1700s refer to 'Forgehouses' in this location, suggesting more than one dwelling, whereas later maps label the property 'Forge House'.

The pool opposite 'Forge Cottage' was originally around twice its present size and was fed by a stream that branched from the Penk across Brewood Park Farm. It was used as a reservoir to drive the waterwheel which in turn operated the forge's bellows

Figure 34: The forge pool today. (Author)

and hammers. The forge building stood immediately beside the road and the tail race fed back into the Penk nearby. An 'overflow' stream was regulated by a weir on the eastern side of the pool, any excess again flowing into the Penk.

By the middle of the nineteenth century such antiquated methods of iron-working had been superseded and the forge became a corn mill. Unfortunately, it was destroyed by fire around 1870, the place thereafter being known as Burnt Mill. James Hicks Smith, in his nineteenth century book about Brewood, suggests that the mill may have been a fulling mill before it became a forge. There are other small pools dotted about nearby which may also be associated with the forge.

Brook House

A building known as 'Brook House' or 'Brooke Houses' appears on the 1861 and 1871 censuses located in the vicinity of Lower Green. This may refer to the cottages that stood near the junction of School Lane and Brewood Road, which belonged to Grange Farm

Figure 35: The recreation ground in the 1950s with Chambley Green under construction in the background. The cottages possibly known as 'Brook Houses' are visible through the goalposts and were demolished in 1973.

and originally provided accommodation for farm labourers, or to what is now known as Brook Cottage, beside the Penk.

Goodacres

During World War II, anti-aircraft guns were located here on Lawn Lane and on 'Middle Lane', immediately south of the present-day M54 motorway, to protect Dowty's aircraft works.

Heath House & Old Heath House

Around the time of the English Civil War, a Mr Nechells bequeathed about 19 acres of land known as 'Green Fields' at Coven Heath in trust. The deed stipulated that the rental income was to be used to maintain the pavements of Wolverhampton and by 1834 the land was bringing in the tidy sum of £40 per annum. The land is thought to have passed from Bushbury parish to the local council sometime thereafter. It is quite possible that this is the same piece of land

Figure 36: Old Heath House today. (Author)

named as 'Greenfield' in a deed dated 1307 and the present-day allotments at Coven Heath, next to 'Old Heath House' may be part of this parcel of land.

Two plots of arable land near Heath House, known as 'Upper Ground' (or 'Far Ground'), were sold at an auction held at the Swan Hotel, Wolverhampton in 1875.

Heath House stood immediately south of the Ball Inn. In 1835, Mr Richard Rolliston and his new wife Elizabeth occupied the house although they did not remain there long as five years later another newly-wed couple, 31-year-old farmer Henry Towers and his wife, were residing there. Mrs Towers was the daughter of Edward Thorneycroft, a Wolverhampton iron-master, whose twin brother Edward was the first mayor of Wolverhampton. From the 1850s, Edward Willington, a wealthy single man who owned a number of fields in the village, lived at Brinsford and Coven Heath, including a spell at Heath House. In 1881, widow Ann Thompson and her son lived at Heath House, neither had an occupation so were presumably living on their own means.

Old Heath House is an imposing late Georgian dwelling standing north of the former Ball Inn. Unlike Heath House, the building doesn't seem to be named on any maps so it may have adopted the name after Heath House disappeared.

William Schoolbred was born in Fife, Scotland in 1795 but came to the Wolverhampton area as a young man along with his brother Robert and the pair ran a tailors shop at Dudley Street, Wolverhampton. In 1840 he purchased part of Charles Mander's business and set himself up in the japanning trade.

William went into partnership with Henry Loveridge and the pair set up a brick-making works in the town and expanded their metalworking business to include tinware and cast iron products. Schoolbred's son, also William, was a partner in the business for a while but he died in 1860.

At the 1851 census, William senior was listed as a tailor and draper living at Coven Heath, most probably at Old Heath House. His wife died in 1873, but William himself lived until 1882, by which time he had reached the age of eighty seven. In the last years of his life he lived at St Ann Villa, Newbridge, along with his sister, a spinster four years his junior. Loveridge's business went on to become one of the largest japanning firms in the country.

By the 1880s Edward Willington, mentioned above, seems to have moved from Heath House to Old Heath House. The Kay family, whose transport business is on the Old Stafford Road, lived at Old Heath House in the 1950s.[10]

Clewley

A track connecting Pendeford Hall to the Old Mill at Coven Heath was once known as Middle Lane. It is thought to be part of the route that Charles took to Moseley Old Hall after leaving Boscobel.

Middle Lane was crossed by another track, running from Wobaston to Coven Lawn, and a farmstead known as Clewley lay just south of this crossroads. No trace of the house remains today but a pool that was adjacent to the property is still there and former field boundaries around the farm can be clearly seen on aerial photographs. The house was built at some time before 1770 and was still in existence in 1927.

The area either side of the former house is now being developed

Figure 37: Pool near the former house known as Clewley. (Author)

into a major business park, although the site itself is designated a scheduled ancient monument and therefore protected. On the original Ordnance Survey maps the dwelling was referred to as 'Pendeford Cottage' but the original name at least lives on in Clewley Drive, Pendeford.[11]

Pendeford Cottage & Brook Cottage

Pendeford Cottage (or cottages) stood in the corner of a field, near to the track from The Hattons to Lower Pendeford Farm, just east of the bridge over the Penk. The cottage was in existence at the time the first Ordnance Survey maps were drawn up and was occupied until the middle of the twentieth century. Electricity supplies were laid past this and nearby Brook Cottage around 1923 but the latter was said to have had no main supplies of any kind when redevelopment was recently considered.

A Mrs Haden lived at Pendeford Cottage in 1830 and at the time of the 1851 census, 55-year-old spinster Sarah Fowler was the sole occupant. Described as a 'land proprietor', she was probably the

Figure 38: Derelict Brook Cottage, shortly before demolition. (Author)

sister of Thomas Fowler, the owner of Pendeford Hall, who died in that same year, and possibly the grand-daughter of another Sarah Fowler, daughter of Richard, who died in 1784.

Brook Cottage was built on the opposite side of the Penk to Pendeford Cottage some time after 1840. It stood derelict for many years at the end of the twentieth century and was finally demolished around 2013.[12]

The Rookery

A postcard photograph of about 1910 shows a range of low cottages known as The Rookery, opposite the 'Harrows' at Standeford. The term 'rookeries' was sometimes used when referring to city slums in the Victorian era but this location was considered idyllic by the person who sent the postcard.

The rightmost three cottages are still standing but those at the left were demolished during road widening. The whole building was

Figure 39: The Rookery around 1910. (Author's collection)

L-shaped, with a return on the east side consisting of another two cottages. There was a guide post at the junction of School Lane and the old Stafford Road, near to the position of the photographer, and a well lay just to the left of the cottages from this viewpoint.

The shop in the picture was run by Arthur Whatton, originally from Bilston, who also ran a refreshment room and seems to have offered accommodation, as the back of the postcard reads:

> "... I do wish you were here it's lovely, this is the house where we are staying....".

Whatton was assisted in the business by his wife Gertrude and they had a son Cecil. They are probably the three people standing immediately in front of the shop in the photograph. The other cottages were at this time mostly occupied by farm, road and rail labourers.

About a century before this photograph was taken, the area in front of the cottages was used to cultivate willows, the land being owned by Mr Shenstone at the mill opposite, and let to numerous individuals, possibly the occupants of The Rookery themselves. The

Figure 40: The Woodlands, at right, on Lower Green.

long field at the rear of these cottages, still pasture-land today, was know as 'Upper Brickkiln Field'.

The Woodlands

This substantial house lay at the south-eastern end of the row of cottages at Lower Green. In 1899 coal merchant Frederick Hill lived there but his business failed and two years later the house was occupied by the Deakins, one of whom married into the Bickford family.

The cottages themselves are still in existence but The Woodlands has long since disappeared. The cottage beside the Woodlands had its 'front door' down the narrow passageway between the two buildings - a common arrangement with town houses but less so in villages.

On some older maps, Lower Green is also referred to as Gregory's Green. The name may be three or more centuries old as a Richard Gregory noted in Brewood parish registers, was living at Coven in the 1620s.[13]

Figure 41: Standeford Lodge, seen here in the 1980s, has recently been refurbished.

Standeford Lodge

In the first decade of the twentieth century, this was the home of Stephen Kirk who ran a butchery business from the adjacent building. The property next to Standeford Lodge is now known as 'Old Cottage'.

Standeford Cottage

There are four houses that are or have been called Standeford Cottage. Firstly, the building today known as 'White Lodge' is referred to as 'Standeford Cottage' on maps of the late nineteenth century.

Secondly, one of the cottages on the opposite side of the road and nearer to Standeford Mill is now known as 'Standeford Cottage',

Figure 42: Cottage opposite the mill, around 1980, now known as The Mill Cottage.

the adjoining one being Wayside Cottage. Next, the cottage directly opposite Standeford Mill may have carried the name - that building is believed to have housed a lock-smith's workshop and William Cox, a lock manufacturer with a Wolverhampton factory, is known to have lived at a 'Standeford Cottage' at the time of his death around 1865.

Finally, what is now the end house in the row of cottages opposite the Harrows is also currently named 'Standeford Cottage'.

A house and petrol station at Standeford was built by William Simms on land that once belonged to Grange Farm. This developed into the present-day 'K Transport' depot. The footpath running from Light Ash to the Old Stafford Road originally ran directly to White Lodge and hence the canal - it was later diverted to emerge north of this industrial development.[14]

Figure 43: Wayside Cottage around the middle of the twentieth century.

Caravan Parks

There have been a number of caravan and mobile home parks in the area over the last sixty years, during which time some have grown and others have shrunk or disappeared altogether. There was much discussion of the matter in the 1960s when it was said that two thirds of Coven's population lived in caravans! There were a number of reasons for this situation, not least that it was difficult to obtain a council house in the area. It was also cheaper than buying or renting a house, especially for young families and older people.

There were those strongly in favour of the situation, particularly shop-keepers and employers who benefited from the increased headcount, and those who worried that the parks were changing the character of the area and putting extra pressures on housing stock, education and welfare services. Over time the parks have become part of the fabric of the village, where people can live economically

Figure 44: Darelyn Caravan Park, owned by Frank Till, offered economical living in pleasant environment. (M. Nicholls)

but in an out-of-town environment.

Part of the 'Star Mobile Home Park' occupies the northern end of a field once known as 'Great Meadow' and the large, roughly triangular, field south of the park was originally two fields, 'Broad & Kempson Meadows'.

Chapter 2
Mills and Farms

In the Middle Ages, villages such as Coven operated the 'open field system', where a few very large fields near the village were divided into long strips, groups of which were farmed by individual tenants or families. Villagers didn't own these strips of land but they had the right to work them and this entitlement would be passed down to their descendants. Livestock was kept on common meadow or waste ground but were also allowed to graze the open fields after the harvest was brought in.

In the late medieval period the number of sheep being farmed in England increased greatly, wool having become a significant driver of the English economy. This change in farming practice, along with the beginnings of mechanisation and improvements in agricultural science, precipitated the enclosure of land into large rectangular fields, often resulting in the eviction of tenants and the loss of common grazing. This aggregation, enabled by buying-up rights or by Parliamentary Act, concentrated ownership in a small number of individuals and families.

Most of the land around Coven has been in the hands of two families since the late Middle Ages, the Giffards of Chillington and, slightly more recently, the Moncktons of Stretton. During the nineteenth century there were still a few minor landowners, most of whom were farmers working their own land and sometimes that belonging to one of the aforementioned landlords or each other. Some of these farming families, such as the Richards, Chambleys,

Bickfords, Kirks and Smiths, worked the same land for several generations and were influential in their community, helping to shape the area we know today in many different ways.

Up until the early nineteenth century, when there was still no church or school in the immediate vicinity, the 'built environment' consisted of these farms and their outbuildings, a small number of dwellings and workshops, a few public houses and a couple of mills.

Mills of one form or another have been an integral part of village life for many centuries. Watermills existed in Roman Britain, became widespread after the eleventh century and continued to operate in the same essential form until the beginning of the modern era. The rotary motion of a waterwheel could be adapted by the use of simple gearing, cams or belts to accomplish many different tasks, from the essential grinding of corn, to the fulling of wool. Further modifications enabled the mechanisation of hammers and bellows for use in the iron smelting and working processes, the sharpening of blades, the grinding of bone for fertilizer, and a variety of sawing, stamping and rolling operations on all manner of raw materials.

Windmills began to be used in Europe in the Medieval period. Unlike a water-powered mill, there was no way to create a reserve of power so a windmill could only operate when conditions were right. During the Middle Ages there were probably a few hundred windmills in operation at any one time, compared to many thousands of watermills. Nevertheless, they could provide a useful alternative in areas that had no suitable water supply or were prone to windy conditions.

Coven Heath Old Mill & Windmill

Robert Plot, the 17th century author of 'The Natural History of Staffordshire', noted a particular type of clay found in the vicinity of Coven Heath which was believed to have medicinal properties. He also recounts that many curious pebbles had been found in the area. Some time after this an attempt was made to set up an emery mill, where suitable types of rock could be ground into an abrasive powder, but the venture was not successful. In the middle of the nineteenth century the British Association for the Advancement of Science also noted that some of the pebbles here were transparent, "extremely hard and glitter almost as much as diamond".

In 1774 Richard and Elizabeth Slater took a mortgage on property and land at Coven Heath from James Aston, a locksmith of Brinsford, but five years later the now widowed Mrs Slater and her son surrendered the property. At about this time William Price of The Laches also owned an estate at Coven Heath. Either of these could have included the land on which the mill stood.

Court proceedings in 1801 mention Coven Mill House, the water-powered corn mill, a windmill and several adjacent fields: Mill Hayes (otherwise known as Horse Leasow), Mill Hayes Meadow (otherwise known as Nether Meadow), the Heathy Leasow and the Kiln House Piece. At this time another dwelling at Coven Heath, known as Day's Farm, belonged to the canal company. In 1834, Richard Brooke contributed 15 shillings each year to the Wolverhampton 'doles', from rental income he received in respect of Mill Hayes.

The old watermill had been in existence since at least 1610 (when it was owned by Sampson Oginton) but had fallen out of use by the 1860s, at which time the building served as a farmhouse for William Clifft. Later in that century the Old Mill became a 'sewage farm', where attempts were made to process waste from the ever-expanding population of Wolverhampton.

The windmill at Coven Heath stood in the field at the junction of Shaw Hall Lane and Ball Lane as early as 1775. Another at Somerford, in the field between Claygate Road and Crateford Lane, was in existence from 1802 or earlier until at least 1852. These windmills may each have been constructed a century or more before these dates - that in a superior position at Essington was built in 1681. The windmills at Essington and Somerford were 'post windmills', the earliest type, where the entire structure was mounted on a single post, allowing it to be rotated into the wind as required.

On Thursday 28th January 1802 gale force winds, said to be the worst in living memory, raged across much of England. During this storm the windmill at Coven Heath was completely blown down and part of the watermill at Pendeford was also demolished. It seems likely that the windmill was not rebuilt, as it does not appear on later maps, and is somewhat ironic that it was destroyed by that which it was designed to harvest!

During excavations at the sewage works in the 1960s, parts of a small 'gin mill' were found - this simple, horse-powered device was probably used to grind corn.[15]

Standeford Mill

There was a mill at Standeford, possibly in the same location as the later mill, as early as the fourteenth century. The mill is marked on William Yates' map of 1775, but the original building was added to in the middle of the nineteenth century. For most of its working life it was a corn mill but in its final three or four decades was used for grinding horse fodder. The mill ceased to operate in the 1930s and its buildings were later modernised and converted for residential use and the millpond filled in. Deepmore Mill, which lay about a mile up-stream of Standeford, was a corn and blade mill (employed to sharpen tool blades) and is thought to be the older of the two.

When in use, the pond at the back of the property was supplied with water from Saredon Brook. After turning the water-wheel, the mill race fed back into the brook a little further downstream, near Standeford bridge. A wooden footbridge led from the back of the house across the mill pool, which was surrounded by attractive gardens.

From at least 1818 until early 1834, William Shenstone was the

Figure 45: Mill pond and gardens at Standeford

corn miller and maltster at Standeford. John Shenstone Austin took over the mill and ran it until the middle years of the century. He died in 1864 and his impressive tombstone can be seen near the gate at St Paul's church.

In the late 1860s Michael Wedge was the miller, farmer and maltster at Standeford. In 1868 his wife was having trouble finding servants - she advertised on at least three occasions for a nursery governess, a cook and a domestic servant. Previous applicants were told not to re-apply; perhaps her four children, all aged under 12, were just too much to handle!

Richard Pullen ran the mill in the last decades of the century, followed by his son John. Richard retired to Standeford Cottage where he died in September 1895 - his grave can be seen at St Paul's. At some point the mill passed to the Yeomans family who subsequently sold it to the Monckton estate. Clara Pullen, a middle-aged widow, lived at Four Ashes around the turn of the century. Her son, who was a brewer, was christened Richard Standeford Pullen. He went on to serve in the First World War, achieving the rank of

Figure 46: Coven Farm around 1930.

Lieutenant in the South Staffordshire Regiment but was killed in action during October 1917.

In the 1933, when Mr Cowern lived there, the mill was severely damaged by a night-time fire - traffic had to be diverted away from the Old Stafford Road for several hours until the blaze was brought under control.

Often-visited buildings, such as mills, usually acquired a direct route from nearby habitation and Standeford Mill was no exception. A footpath from Church Alley ran to Light Ash and onwards directly to the mill. The path remains today but, being bisected by the A449, its original purpose is not immediately obvious.[16]

Coven Farm

This house is thought to have been built in the late Elizabethan period and bears the date '1600'. It seems likely that 'Mr Nicholls', named as the farmer here at the turn of the eighteenth century, was actually Mr *Nickolds*, whose son Titus was running Coven Farm forty years later. Titus Nickolds' young wife and baby were buried at St Mary & St Chad, Brewood towards the end of that decade.

There were about twenty fields attached to the farm at that time, including the charmingly named 'Field Before The Door' and the 'Great Hutts' and 'Little Hutts', these two possibly taking their name from the Old English word for a projecting piece of ground. Perhaps most interesting, and harking back to the earliest days of the farm is land described as 'two moietys in great old Furlong'. This refers to two shares (i.e. strips, or groups of strips) in a large field, farmed under the open-field system before wholesale enclosure began.

At the start of the next century, George John Parkes was a butcher at Standeford Lodge but his business failed. Stephen Kirk subsequently ran a butchery from the same property but he sold the business to Joe Simms who transferred it to Coven Farm in 1938. The start of the twentieth century does not seem to have been a good time for local butchers, as a year before Parkes went out of business, Charles Coley of Light Ash, previously a farmer and pork butcher at Coven Heath was also declared bankrupt.

The low buildings beside Coven Farm were originally pigsties but now accommodate two businesses, a butchers and a book shop, the latter having been a hardware and building supplies store beforehand.[17]

Three Hammers Farm

As mentioned elsewhere, Three Hammers was farmed in the early 19th century by John Smith senior, who was also a maltster (one who prepared barley for brewing) and an engineer! The farm was in existence at least fifty years before this time however. Smith and his son worked on their inventions and improvements for farm machinery here before the opening of their foundry in the centre of the village.

The large farmhouse stood where the gated housing developments now stands, just south of the start of the Old Stafford Road. There were outbuildings on the north and east sides of the farmhouse and the farm had its own well, close to the brook that passes

Figure 47: Coven farm in the second half of the twentieth century. (M. Nicholls)

Figure 48: The pigsties at Coven Farm.

Figure 49: Looking towards the centre of the village from Coven Farm. Parker's Place at right is the only building still in existence, the others were demolished in the mid 1960s or earlier.

under the Stafford Road. A footpath ran from the farm, directly across 'Careless Field', now the golf course, into Coven. The name of the farm may derive from the old word 'Hammes', meaning pastures, rather than being anything to do with metalworking.

In 1841 engineer Joseph Yates lived at the Three Hammers, perhaps he was in some way involved in Smith's business. In 1871 the Three Hammers was farmed by Charles Smith but ten years later farm bailiff Felix Day lived there, suggesting that it had either ceased to be a farm or that the land was being farmed by someone else. During the 19th and 20th centuries the Three Hammers was owned by the Legge family (i.e. the Earl of Dartmouth of Patshull Hall) and Lady Joan Margaret Legge lived at the farm during the 1930s. Dick Whalley bough the site from the Legges in the 1940s and developed the golf course in the 1960s - the triangular patch of ground between the old Stafford Road and the canal, now occupied by the golf centre and driving range, was owned by Edward Willington and known as 'Rickyard Leasow' in John Smith's time.

Figure 50: Three Hammers Farm with sheep on what is now the golf course. The barn at left carried the landmark 'Whalley's White Potatoes' sign. (M. Nicholls)

Coven Heath Wood, a little south of the farm and lying in the angle between the Stafford Road and the canal, was some 4 acres in extent at the end of the 19th century.

Grange Farm

The original Grange farmhouse was constructed in the late 1500s and added to over the following centuries. It has been 're-styled' on at least three occasions during the last century; doorways, chimneys, external rendering and garden have all been changed. The building has much original timber inside and out and a panelled bedroom with a 'priest-hole'. It has an unusual diagonal 'dragon beam' supporting the jettied first floor and the original chimneys had a typical black diamond pattern in the brickwork.

The farm was probably occupied by the Illedge family during the eighteenth century and may have been in the same family for a hundred years or more. At least two generations of the Cliffts farmed here for much of the nineteenth century. In the 1920s Mr

Figure 51: Cottages at the former Three Hammers Farm, 2013. (Author)

Horton was the farmer and in the 1950s the farm was owned by Wolverhampton and Dudley Breweries and occupied by Mr and Mrs Proudley and family.

The small square field at immediately behind the Grange was known as 'Bowling Green Piece' ('Bowling Alley Piece' being at the top end of School Lane) and at the end of the 1700s some of the farm's other fields were 'Field Against The Lane' and 'Rush Croft'.

Lawn Farm

Lawn Farm stood at the top end of Coven Lawn, a wide grassy stretch of land forming the centre section of what is now Lawn Lane. Around the start of the nineteenth century, the total area of the Lawn was given as eight acres. Given that it was no more than 1.5 kilometres in length it must have had an average width of around twenty metres! By contrast, the common 'green' at Cross Green was just over three acres.

Figure 52: This 1912 postcard view of Grange Farm shows the older (rightmost) part of the building to good effect.

Figure 53: A postcard view of the property in its 'black and white' phase around 1940.

There was a farmhouse here from at least 1775 and farming continued for over two centuries until the house and barns were put to purely residential use. With an estate totalling just over 130 acres, the farm was second in size only to Brewood Park.

A piece of meadow land in Coven, possibly at Coven Lawn was known as 'Cold Lawn Meadow' - in 1729 it was mentioned in the will of one Richard Moon, the rental income of £5 going to the poor of the parish. There were other such benefactions in the area, for example, at some point before 1836, a Mr Dobson donated a piece of land immediately south of Standeford Bridge to the church, the rent to be paid to the poor of Wolverhampton and Tettenhall.

Joseph Robinson and his wife Mary lived at Coven Lawn in 1794 but whether he was the farmer here is uncertain. His wife seems to have died in childbirth aged just 22 - she and the infant are buried at St Mary & St Chad, Brewood, the gravestone can still be clearly read.

In early 1797 William Bassett (or possibly his heirs) put up for auction an area of land along Lawn Lane, known as the Rye Leasows. The land was used for grazing and growing timber, the auction being held at the Crown Inn, Cannock.

A small sub-triangular plot of land south west of Lawn Farm and beside the River Penk was in the possession of the Bushbury Poor before 1840 but most of the land between Lawn Lane and the river was owned by the Monckton estate. Thomas Bate was the farmer in the 1840s although he had lived at a cottage on the opposite side of the Lawn a little further south at the start of that century.

William Gripton farmed the land in the 1880s; he and his wife are also buried at St Mary & St Chad, Brewood.

Just before the First World War, Joseph Cooper was the farmer, assisted by his son and two daughters, one of whom worked in the dairy. Mr Cooper also served the community as a Justice of the Peace. In the 1930s Mr Batchelor was the farmer.

Until the twentieth century, the field known as 'Adderholes', nearest the confluence of Watershead Brook and the River Penk seems to have been more undulant but has now been evened out by

Figure 54: Lawn Farm around 1980.

Figure 55: Poplars Farm, looking towards the Bront and, in the distance, houses on Brewood Road. (M. Nicholls)

ploughing.[18]

Poplars Farm

The fields attached to Poplars Farm lay to the south west of the farmhouse. In the eighteenth century this land was owned by William Chambley but shortly after the First World War it belonged to a Mrs Woodcock.

Charles Kench farmed here in the twentieth century, having lived at Slade Heath as a young man. He is said to have delivered milk by putting the churns in his motorcycle side-car! Mr and Mrs Adams ran a pig farm here until about 1970, after which the house stood derelict for a number of years until it was refurbished. Coven's Great War memorial was positioned on the side of the cottage, until the new one was consecrated in 1982 beside the Memorial Hall. The outline of the old monument is still visible beneath the white rendered finish on the side of the building.

Figure 56: The War Memorial on Poplars Farm Cottage, c. 1940. (Author's collection)

Figure 57: Outline of War Memorial, 2013. (Author)

Paradise and Manor Farms

Manor Farm lay on the east side of Paradise Lane, while Paradise Farm lay on the west.

The properties are said to have been in the Bickford family for 400 years or more; in 1643 Henry Bickford of The Laches is mentioned in Brewood parish registers and 'Paradice Cottage', possibly the original Paradise or Manor farmhouse, is mentioned in the will of Henry Richards dated 1669.

The Bickford family owned other properties around Coven at various times, for example Oaklands Cottage, the Harrows and the Anchor. Most of the land between Paradise and Cross Green was farmed by the Bickford, Chambley, or Smith families. It was not uncommon however for Smith to be farming fields owned by Chambley, for example, and vice versa.

William Bickford, who took over the farm from his parents at the end of the nineteenth century, was a keen breeder and exhibitor of cattle. He entered many of his cows into contests, taking prizes with "Rosedale Fairy" and "Millionaire", amongst others, the latter no doubt being so named because it was bred by Baron Rothschild!

There was a large ornamental pool on the north side of Manor Farm and the 3.5 acre field at the rear became an orchard in the early decades of the 20th century - in the late 1930s it was producing as much as thirty tons of apples at each harvest. A small cottage that stood opposite provided accommodation for farm labourers.

The original Manor House was probably a half-timbered building; the kitchen displayed original oak beams and more were exposed during demolition of the building in 1971.

Two stone lions above the portico to Paradise Farm were taken by relatives to their house in Church Lane when the building was demolished in the 1960s. This is not the only garden in Coven to be embellished with artefacts - after alterations to Brewood parish church in 1827, the font was removed to a garden in Coven!

Land belonging to the farm was requisitioned during World War II for the construction of a Royal Ordnance Factory. This substantial munitions facility had a rail connection and its own steam lo-

Figure 58: Manor House in the early 20th century. (L. Dutton)

Figure 59: Manor Farm. The building at right was a small cottage, on the diagonally opposite side of the crossroads. (L. Dutton)

Figure 60: Derelict outbuildings at Manor Farm in 2005, almost all had gone by 2014. (Author)

Figure 61: Paradise farmhouse. (L. Dutton)

Figure 62: Looking along Paradise Lane towards the crossroads, with a car parked outside Manor Farm on the right. (L. Dutton)

comotives for shunting in the sidings. It stood until around 1964 when the prison was constructed on the site. Bickford's lorry depot now stands on the site of Paradise Farm itself.

Around 1840 William Bickford was living at a house immediately beside the new railway, on the east side of the bridge over Brinsford Lane. The house had been in existence for at least seventy years and another house stood nearby, at the south end of Paradise Lane, which was occupied by the Simpson family. The two fields immediately south of *that* property were known as 'Poors Meadow' and 'Poors Land', held by the church but farmed by Mr Chambley.[19]

Barr Farm

Richard Lovatt was the farmer here up until his death in 1830 at the age of 79. His widow Sarah seems to have continued until their son, also Richard, took over the reins. The tithe map notes a malthouse here and the largest field at the rear of the property had the interesting name 'Near Irelands'. In the first decade of the twentieth century, Henry Bickford was the farmer here.

Bridge Farm

Located on the opposite (south) side of the canal to Coven Heath Wood, this farm was in existence as early as 1775. A bungalow and works now occupy the site.

In 1920 it was occupied by a Mr Holmes. Considering its position beside a main road it is hard to believe that the property had no electricity until around 1960; up until this time it relied solely upon gas lighting.

Brinsford Farm

A lease of 1710 details a house with outhouses, barns and stables at Brinsford, owned by Anne Kempson of Essington and several members of the famous Pendrell family. By 1728 widow Kempson had died and a new lease seems to have come into effect, the lessee being one Henry Slater, a brass founder. The lease included two small fields beside the house, four arable fields and a meadow.

There are many legal documents spanning the period 1750-1800 which may relate to this house and the surrounding land; these may be inspected at Wolverhampton Archives.

Around the time of the Great War a Mr Moreton lived here but it seems to have been in the Price family, who also farmed at Featherstone, for most of the years since. Enclosures totalling over 30 acres alongside nearby Paradise Lane, but now beneath the new prison, were known as 'Brand's Heath'.[20]

Aspley Farm

Aspley was built in the early 16th century as a moated, timber-framed open hall and was divided into upper and lower storeys about a century later.

Figure 63: Aspley Farm in the 1980s. (S. Caton)

Charles Wade lived at Aspley in the first decade or so of the nineteenth century. His wife died just eight days after the birth of their son, Charles Joseph, in 1816. The younger Charles became a barrister and was the Liberal Party candidate for East Devon in 1868. He later became a magistrate and owned a farm near Newton Abbot, Devon. By the 1830s the hall had become a farmhouse occupied by Michael Lovatt, most likely son of the Michael Lovatt who died at Barr Farm in 1830.

In the middle of the century James Perkin was the farmer and at some point Aspley became a dairy farm before being returned to mixed use. Jonah Wootton was the farmer in 1911.

In 1851 a building known as 'Railway House' lay somewhere between Aspley Cottage and the Black Lion - possibly on the site of the house that now has gated access beneath the railway.[21]

Brewood Park Farm

There were three deer parks in this part of Staffordshire in the Medieval period; one at Hilton, another at Chillington and a third right beside the village, at what is now Brewood Park Farm. This latter park is believed to have been established around the year 1200, and is said to have been hunted by King John, whose itinerary occasionally took in Brewood. In the post-Medieval period, the park was owned by the Giffard family of Chillington and they continued as owners until a century or so after the land was converted to agricultural use around 1800.

William Walhouse, "of the Parke", mentioned in the Brewood parish registers in 1614, was most likely a park keeper and the history of the land was brought vividly to life when a calcified antler was found on the land in the twentieth century. The artefact was discovered by Basil Warrington, who worked on the farm and lived at Brewood Park Cottages.

In 1647, it was said that the nearby ironworks would advance the sale of wood from Brewood Park and that the land would yield good corn if ploughed, but the enclosed park continued to appear on various maps until at least 1722 and must therefore have been converted to agricultural use after that date. No farmhouse is shown on William Yates' map of 1775, although the land itself may have been under the plough by then. In any event, enclosure and division of fields clearly happened before the Shropshire Union canal was built in the early 1830s.

The farmhouse itself retains many period features, including an intact bell-pull board; when rung the bells would each sound a different tone, so that servants would know in which room they were required. The house has an original marble fireplace, substantial cellars and an attractive wooden staircase. A corner cupboard in one room is said to have come from the Four Ashes Inn, as are the railings protecting the external steps to the cellar.

Cart sheds beside the house were cleared away in the middle of the twentieth century, a lawn and garden being put in their place, but otherwise the house is little altered externally from its original

Figure 64: Antler found at Brewood Park Farm. (Author)

Figure 65: The farmhouse at Brewood Park Farm around 1938. (S.D. Kirk)

Figure 66: Frederick J Keeling farmed at Brewood Park for almost thirty years. (D. Cooper)

form. Sandstone for a substantial outbuilding in the farmyard may have come from Stradsfield quarry on the perimeter of the farm, or from its own 'Quarry Leasow' field. There is an ordnance survey 'benchmark' cut into the wall of the former stables.

Joseph Smith who, was paying rent on some 486 acres of land in 1811, was probably one of the first farmers at Brewood Park. From around 1833 Joseph Wilson was the tenant and his wife Elizabeth continued at the farm for some years after his death in 1844. The Wilson family grave can be seen at St Mary & St Chad, Brewood.

Over the following thirty years Brewood Park Farm had a number of different tenants including Samuel Reynolds, Thomas Watkins, William Bishton and Thomas Atkins.

Frederick J Keeling, descendant of a wealthy farming family from Congreve near Penkridge, was a farmer and miller at Somerford before moving to Brewood Park Farm in 1874. The Keelings had ten children and employed over a dozen people. Of the Keeling's four sons, one was accidentally shot and killed on the driveway to the farm in 1895 and another became a big-game hunter in Kenya, before settling in Canada where his descendants still live.

One of Mr Keeling's daughters had connections to a school in Schwerin in northern Germany and in 1899 she placed the following press advertisement on behalf of the establishment:

> A Lady thoroughly recommends a HIGH CLASS SCHOOL for Young Ladies. Exceptional educational advantages. Resident French governess; healthy neighbourhood; home comforts; good references. - Prospectuses forwarded by Miss Keeling, The Park, Coven, Staffs.

Frederick Keeling's wife, Lucy, died in the winter of 1898 while walking back to the farm from Brewood in deep snow. In 1902, Mr Keeling was looking to recruit a new shepherd - a cottage with garden was available for the successful applicant - but very soon after this he retired to Penkridge, where he lived until 1911. In addition to a long farming career, he undertook various civic duties, including roles as a school governor and church-warden. A commemorative window dedicated to Frederick Keeling can be seen at St Mary & St Chad, Brewood.

George Davies was the last tenant of the Giffards, being there for a little over a decade until the farm was sold in 1918. The grave of Mr Davies and his wife can be seen at St Paul's.

The farm was bought by Joseph Smith of Brades Village, Oldbury. 'Old Joe' Smith and his family owned, and worked in, a hammer factory at Oldbury. He had no interest in the farm other than for recreational shooting, preferring instead to live at 'The Woodlands', Lower Green and letting out the farm to Charles White.

Sidney Kirk took over the farm in 1929, but there was a disagreement between tenant and landlord. Mr Smith's letting agent had promised that an electricity supply would be installed but Smith later decided that it was an unnecessary expense. Mr Kirk then tried to buy the farm, but the relationship between the two men had deteriorated to such an extent that Smith refused to sell it,

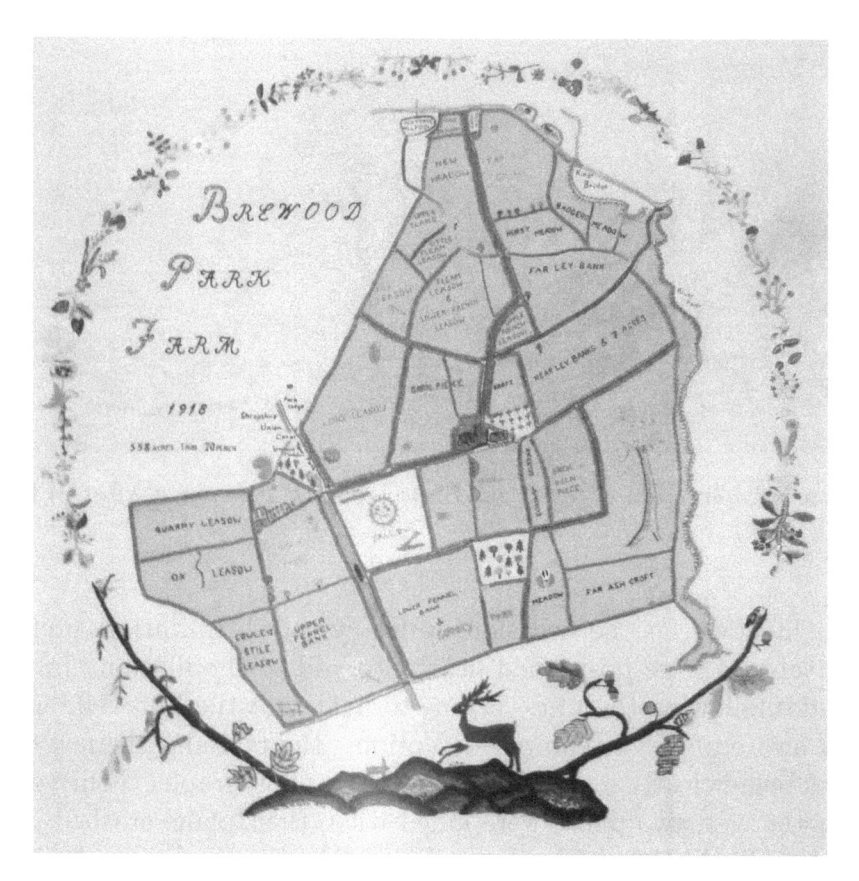

Figure 67: An embroidery showing the farm's fields in 1918 (W. Kirk)

despite the fact that he wished to divest himself of the property. In the end, Mr Kirk used an intermediary to complete the purchase anonymously and the farm has remained in the family ever since.

Sidney Kirk was a progressive farmer who won much praise from the agricultural community for restoring the land to its former condition; he was also one of the first farmers in the area to employ a combine harvester.

A 'shadow factory'a was erected on the farm during World War II, in the hope that it would confuse German bombers and thereby protect the Boulton Paul aircraft factory at Bilbrook. This sham building was a simple canvas structure, so insubstantial that it was

Figure 68: Tractors at work on Brewood Park Farm just after WW2. (S.D. Kirk)

brought down on one occasion by heavy snow! Imitation aircraft and vehicles were positioned nearby to add to the illusion. In the decades following the war, it came to light that the Luftwaffe were fully aware of the attempted deception - the real and shadow factories being clearly marked on their aerial photographs. Four years after the war, two pilots were killed when their plane crashed into a potato field belonging to Lawn Farm - they were testing a trainer built at the nearby Boulton Paul factory.

Arthur Turner, who lived in a cottage near the old school at Light Ash, worked at the farm for sixty four years - a feat that earned him the Royal Agricultural Society's Long Service Medal. He was just twelve when he began work and was 76 when he finally retired in 1950.

The farm has a number of interesting field names, some of which are listed below. These, and others, are mentioned around 1840, although a few had fallen out of use by the time the farm was sold some eighty years later:

Turnip Leasow
Ox Leasow
Quarry Leasow

Figure 69: Cottages beside the bridge to Brewood Park Farm. Taken in the early 1900s it shows Frank Till with his mother and aunt. (M. Nicholls)

    Thistley Piece
    Far Fleam Leasow (its roughly triangular shape possibly resembling a fleam or blood-letting instrument)
    Badgers Meadow
    Badgers Moors
    Upper French Leasow
    Fleam Leasow
    Sun Fallow
    Upper Fennel Bank
    Cowley's Stile Leasow

    A long thin field, bounded by river and road between Brook Cottages and Jackson's Bridge, was farmed by John Smith in the early nineteenth century. The field is known as 'Gospel Meadow', perhaps hinting at a former use; Smith was, after all, a Methodist preacher and there was no chapel in the village until 1839. Confusingly, Brewood Park Farm also had a small field beside the Penk called 'Paradise'![22]

Mount Pleasant Farm

Charles Olerenshaw farmed here in the first half of the eighteenth century but also rented 'Standeford Meadow' (there were two fields with this name near the Harrows) and part of 'Leeks House Close', where the Penkside development now stands. Before moving to Mount Pleasant, he lived at the cottage beside the Stafford Road north of Four Ashes.

Mr Olerenshaw was succeeded by Moses Yeomans, a 'butcher and farmer of 100 acres' between 1861 and 1881. Mr Yeomans' ancestors farmed at Pennymore Hay on Calf Heath, from where his brothers also bred and showed heavy horses. The graves of Mr Olerenshaw and Mr Yeomans can be seen in St Paul's churchyard, although the headstone of Mr Yeomans' grave is now broken. David Morrison was the farmer at Mount Pleasant when the 1911 census was taken.

Field Names

Almost all fields in agricultural areas have, or at least did have, names, for the obvious reason that it would have been most inconvenient and ambiguous for a farmer to constantly have to refer to "that field over there" or "that little pasture by the river", for example! While many names are mundane, some are unusual or intriguing, though often of unfathomable origin.

There are several fields in the vicinity that share the same essential name, for example there are a number of 'Brickkiln', 'Ash', 'Quarry' and 'Rye' fields, and many have the appellation 'leasow' - an ancient word, common in Staffordshire, meaning rough pasture. There are also a number of fields described simply as 'slang' - this was a commonly used name for long, thin fields, especially when situated beside a river or road. There are also a couple of 'hanging' fields but this name is derived from an Old English word for 'sloping' rather than being related to capital punishment!

The parish tithe maps, drawn up in the 1830s, served to apportion charges in lieu of the ancient system of payment in kind.

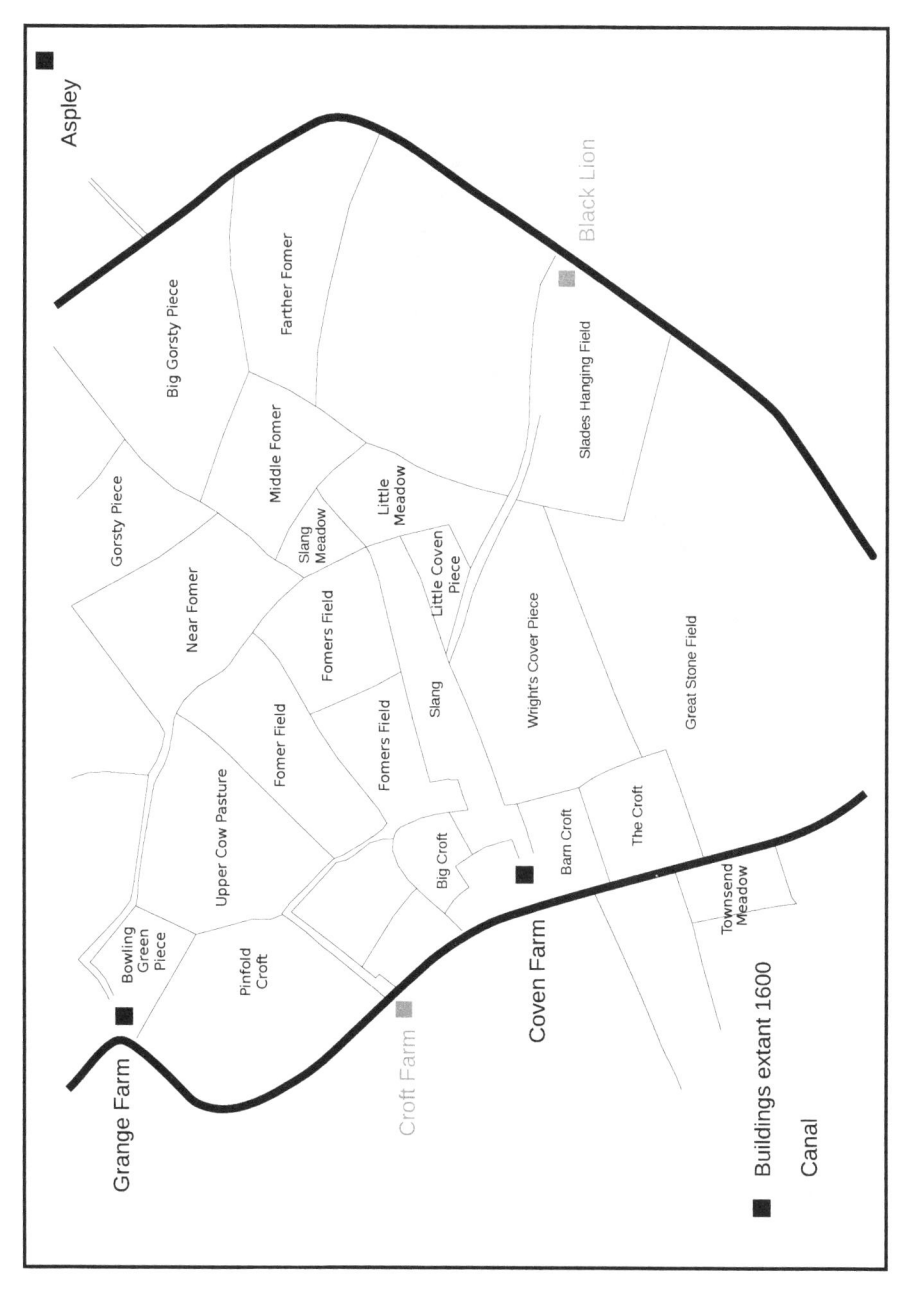

Figure 70: Various 'Fomer' fields lying between Coven and the old Stafford Road circa 1840

The maps were accompanied by detailed schedules which name the land owner, tenant, name, use and size of every field in the parish. Before this point in time, we have to rely on piecemeal information from estate maps, road and canal plans, wills, contracts of sale and so forth.

The longevity of field names can be quite remarkable and it is not unusual to find fields mentioned in the 1600s or earlier having the same name today, although some of the names in the following list of local fields had fallen out of use by the time the tithe map was issued. Names are repeated if they appear in different documents with alternative spellings and other fields that are listed in the tithe apportionments are mentioned elsewhere in the text.

1669
The Homages (probably where The Homage now stands)
Milwoods, Millwards
Broadmeadow Field
Rye Croft (opposite Standeford Lodge or north of Aspley?)
Foulemore Field (see below)
Woodcrofte
Woodcroft Meadow
Wilkes Moore (furlong divided into strips or 'lands', possibly the later 'Wilt's Moor', south east of Lawn Farm)
Bayley (ditto)
Annalt's Meadow
1670
Ritcroft Field
Cold Meadow (off Lawn Lane)
1687
Itchcroft (maybe Ritcroft above, belonging to a house adjoining the street and therefore Coven Farm or Grange Farm)
Milwards Close (beside Itchcroft and the three Milwards below)
Grymsmore Meadow or The Weare Meadow
The Hutts (or Hobcroft) (east of Old Stafford Road near Standeford Lodge)

Leitens Common (probably Light Ash or Leet Each as it was once known)
Pocroft (near Light Ash)
Walker's Croft
Gardenhempbutt (hemp butts refers to rope archery targets)
The Brookyard
Broadmeadow Field (at 'Coven Townsend', south west of The Croft)
Nutcroft (near Cross Green)
Water Ridding (adjoining Brewood Road)
Coldmeadows (off Lawn Lane)
Foomer Field (possibly 'Foulemore Field' above)
1698
Stantiford Meadow (between Standeford Green and Somerford Wood)
Broad Hay Meadows
1710 (all attached to a house at Brinsford)
The Orchard
The Homage
All Teams Croft
The Big Meadow
Greenfield Meadow
The Dairyhouse Piece
The Leasow
Fore Croft
Share Croft
Little Piece
Brook Meadow
Cross Green Piece (near Cross Green)
Corbetts Piece (possibly Corbetts Leasow at Paradise)
1729
Cold Lawn Meadow (as above)
1797
Rye Leasows (at Coven Lawn)
1800 (circa)
Adderholes (beside Lawn Lane)

Brick Kiln Flat (on south side at end of Light Ash)
Great Hutts (as above)
Little Hutts
Black Leasow (west of Shaw Hall Farm)
The Moors In Three Parts (south West of Lawn Farm)
Banky Piece (adjacent to the track from Lawn Farm to Shaw Hall Farm)
Great Lees (north of Lawn Farm beside the lane)
Field Opposite Duncalfes (probably the same as 'Field Opposite Duncombs' mentioned in the tithe apportionment)
Field Before The Door
Higg Meadow (Higgs Meadow in the tithe awards)
Near, Middle & Farther Stocking Brook (..Stocking Birch in the tithe awards)
Shaw Lane Leasow (between Lawn Lane and Shaw Hall Lane)
Broad & Kempson Meadow (probably 'Broadmeadow Field' above)
Field Against The Lane
Rush Croft (on Dark Lane)
Twist Meadow (near Mount Pleasant, at one time belonging to Birch, later Nicholls)
Little Old Furlong

1801
Mill Hayes (at Coven Old Mill)

1802
Townsend Piece (probably 'Townsend Meadow' at the south end of the village)
Gilbert's Piece (south-east of village?)
Little Meadow (beside track to Staffs & Worcs)
Clover Piece
Parsons Croft
William's Meadow
Wier Meadow (as above Weare Meadow)
The Water Iddin (sic but certainly Water Ridding as above)
Rough Meadow (at the Bront)
Little Moor

>The Near Milwards
>The Far Milwards
>The Little Milwards Meadow
>Fomer's Field (see Foomer Field above)[23]

In 1687, Foomer Field was said to be "lately enclosed from a common". It seems likely that Foomer is a contraction of Foulemore, mentioned in 1669, and that the various Foomer/Fomer fields are the post-enclosure remnants of this large piece of common. The word 'Foule' is of French origin, meaning a large group of people. Foulemore (pronounced 'Fool-moor') would therefore indicate a moor used by many, ie a common.

It is interesting to note that the three nearest farms in existence at the start of the seventeenth century, each had more or less direct access to this land:

>Grange Farm via the track into 'Near Foomer'
>Coven Farm via the 'Slang'
>Aspley Farm via its lane and the old Stafford Road

The later farms at the Croft and Black Lion also had easy routes:

>From Croft Farm via what is now Church Lane
>From the Black Lion via what is now the public footpath

Chapter 3
Road, Rail and Water

The paths and tracks that criss-cross our landscape can be much more ancient than the oldest standing buildings. Usually it's possible to discern a clear reason for the existence of a particular path; it might lead to an important place, such as a church, mill or river crossing, skirt difficult ground such as a marsh, hill or thicket, or simply connect two settlements to each other for convenience. Over time, those paths that were of most benefit, and amenable to horse or cart, will have become wider tracks and the most important of these in turn may eventually have become proper roads.

In the modern era, the construction of canals, the railway and finally the dual carriageway, have cut some footpaths around Coven into discrete sections but most can be traced in full and are generally still public rights of way.

The primary route in this area is of course the ancient Stafford road, but its branches westwards to Brewood and eastwards to Featherstone may be of almost equal antiquity. The Roman roads from Greensforge (near Wombourn) and Birmingham, converged near Crateford, just south of 'Pennocrucium', a settlement established at some time before 200 AD on Watling street. These gravel or pebble covered roads, some 25 feet wide, with drainage ditches at either side, must have carried a huge amount of foot and horse traffic during the Roman occupation and rather less as they fell into disrepair over the succeeding centuries.

Closer to the present day, there were many complaints about the state of roads and bridges in this area in the early nineteenth century. Nevertheless, most were good enough to permit the Staffordshire Advertiser to declare in 1802 that they achieved same-day distribution "throughout every town and populous village" of the county.

Although some road maps and many detailed town and field plans existed at this time, the first really accurate maps of the country didn't appear until the middle of that century, when the Ordnance Survey began 'levelling' locations across England in order to produce maps with accurate elevations. This mammoth task involved measuring the exact height, relative to a fixed 'datum point', at a huge number of locations across the entire country.

The points at which measurements were taken in this first survey, sometimes called the 'first geodetic levelling', were marked by cutting 'benchmarks' into the walls of buildings, bridges and other structures, and one of the first routes surveyed followed the road from Stafford to Wolverhampton. Benchmarks are denoted on old Ordnance Survey maps by the letters 'BM' plus the measured height, for example 'BM 312' and there are marks from the original survey and succeeding ones in various places around Coven.

Over the decades this network of benchmarks expanded considerably and they were regularly examined and replaced if damaged or destroyed. With the coming of satellite-based GPS systems, the need for benchmarks has disappeared and the vast majority are therefore no longer maintained. As a consequence, many have disappeared as a result of wear or demolition.

The most notable piece of infrastructure associated with any form of transport is the bridge and there are a surprising number of them in the district, over road, rail, canal and river. However, the requirement that travel be as smooth and swift as possible means that some bridges barely register as such today, that beside The Harrows being a prime example. In the past such bridges were much more prominent features in the local landscape and in people's minds as, in addition to being difficult and expensive to build, they had to be maintained at the expense, and using the labour of, the parish in which they were located.

Not all of the bridges in the area are included here, for example the various railway over-bridges that were all built using the same 'template' and the recently constructed timber footbridge over the Penk at Lower Pendeford.

The Grand Junction Railway

The Grand Junction Railway, which runs through this area, opened in 1837 and was one of the first major railway routes in the world. Of the villages and hamlets described in this book, Four Ashes is the one most directly linked to the railway as there was a station here until 1959, but the entire area has been influenced by it to some degree.

In 1834 the famous railway engineer, George Stephenson, put construction of the line around Penkridge out to tender. The southern end of this section ended near the canal at Slade Heath, "in the township of Coven". Whoever won the construction contract seems to have over-estimated the materials required for the project as in early 1838, a very large quantity of surplus rail, railway construction equipment and other miscellaneous items was sold by auction at Slade Heath.

Although the track is quite flat and straight at the southern end of this section (and therefore rather boring to traverse), Freeling's 'Grand Junction Railway Companion', published shortly after the line opened in 1837, marvelled at the embankment at Standeford, recording it as the highest on the entire line.

A fold-out drawing from a guidebook illustrates a typical train from the earliest years of the Grand Junction railway. Behind the locomotive and tender it shows passenger accommodation with roof luggage and a guard, a carriage transporter and a goods wagon. Early trains had very simple couplings between carriages and passengers were extremely vulnerable in the event of a collision, even at the lowest speeds. Many early trains also had completely open carriages with extremely basic bench-like seating, allowing passengers to experience the weather in the same manner as the driver

GRAND JUNCTION RAILWAY.—To CONTRACTORS.—The Directors are now ready to receive Tenders for the execution and maintenance of a FURTHER PORTION of the LINE, viz. for that part of the Works called " The Penkridge Contract," extending from the Newport and Stafford road, in the township of Forebridge, to a point south of the Staffordshire and Worcestershire Canal, near Slade Heath, in the township of Coven, both in the county of Stafford, a distance of 10¼ miles.

The Specification and Plans, with the Conditions and Form of Tender, may be seen on application at the Company's Offices, Mersey Chambers, Old Church-yard, Liverpool. No Tender will be received after the 1st day of December, 1834.

By order of the Directors,
GEO. STEPHENSON, Engineer.
Liverpool, Oct. 22, 1834.

Figure 71: Advertisement from the Courier of 7th November 1834, inviting tenders for the Penkridge Contract.

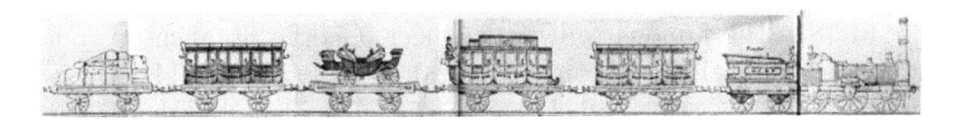

Figure 72: Fold-out picture from a Grand Junction guide book.

and fireman!

Trains such as this, passing by Coven on a daily basis, must initially have been viewed in wonder and no doubt came as a shock to livestock and wildlife nearby. Osbornes 'Guide To The Grand Junction', published just a couple of years after the railway opened, tells us that in this vicinity:

> "The neighbouring country is one of Arcadian tranquillity. The land is in the hands of gentlemen farmers, who richly cultivate it, and adorn it with well-built and pleasantly arranged houses. Fourteen times a day the rushing and clattering engine, with its thundering train, passes rapidly by, putting everything into commotion for a few minutes; but it is soon gone, and leaves no trace behind it; all being as quiet again directly as if no disturbance had ever occurred."

The station building at Four Ashes was similar to that at Penkridge insofar as the ticket office, at platform level, was the middle storey with the stationmaster's residence occupying the lower and upper floors. On the east side of the station was the cattle dock, a fenced-off piece of grassland, that enabled livestock to be loaded or unloaded from trains.

In 1841, John Robinson of Coven Heath was employed solely as a time-keeper for the railway. In these early days, before the advent of signalling, railways operated on a simple interval system whereby trains were only permitted to run at full speed when an earlier train had passed more than ten minutes beforehand. Track-side railway policemen used coloured flags to indicate whether the driver should stop, proceed with caution or continue with full speed ahead. Whether Mr Robinson was involved in this process, in recording train journey times or in keeping station clocks synchronised we cannot tell.

A flavour of what it would be like to travel on the Grand Junction in this era can be gleaned from the company's regulations (quoted here verbatim):

> Time of departure: The doors of the Booking Office are closed precisely at the time appointed for starting, after which no passenger can be admitted.
>
> Booking: There are no Booking Places, except at the Company's Offices at the respective Stations. Each Booking Ticket for the First Class Trains is numbered to correspond with the seat taken. The places by the mixed Trains are not numbered.
>
> Luggage: Each Passenger's Luggage will, as far as practicable, be placed on the roof of the coach in which he has taken his place; carpet bags and small luggage may be placed underneath the seat opposite to that which the owner occupies. No charge for bona fide luggage belonging to the passenger under 100lb. weight; above that weight, a charge is made at the rate of 1d. per lb. for the whole distance. No kind of merchandise

allowed to be taken as luggage. The attention of travellers is requested to the legal notice exhibited at the different stations, respecting the limitation of the Company's liabilities to the loss or damage of luggage. All passengers by Railway will do well to have their luggage distinctly marked with their names and destination.

Gentlemen's carriages and horses: Gentlemen's carriages and horses must be at the Stations at least a quarter of an hour before the time of departure. A supply of trucks are kept at all the principal Stations on the line; but to prevent disappointment it is recommended that previous notice should be given, when practicable, at the Station where they may be required. No charge for landing or embarking carriages or horses on any part of the line.

Road stations: Passengers intending to join the Trains at any of the stopping places are desired to be in good time, as the train will leave each Station as soon as ready, without reference to the time stated in the tables, the main object being to perform the whole journey as expeditiously as possible. Passengers will be booked only conditionally upon there being room on the arrival of the Trains, and they will have the preference of seats in the order in which they are booked. No persons are booked after the arrival of the Train. All persons are requested to get into and alight from the coaches invariably on the left side, as the only certain means of preventing accidents from Trains passing in an opposite direction.

Conductors, guards, and Porters: Every Train is provided with Guards, and a Conductor, who is responsible for the order and regularity of the journey. The Company's Porters will load and unload the luggage, and put it into or upon any omnibus or other carriage at any of the Stations. No fees or gratuities allowed to be received by the Conductors, Guards, Porters, or other persons in the service of the Company.

Smoking, selling of liquors, &c: No smoking is allowed in the Station-houses, or in any of the coaches, even with the consent of the passengers. A substantial breakfast may be had at the Station-house at Birmingham, by parties, going by the early train; but no person is allowed to sell liquors or eatables of any kind upon the line. The Company earnestly hope that the public will co-operate with them in enforcing this regulation, as it will be the means of removing a cause of delay, and will greatly diminish the chance of accident.

Goods sent to Birmingham, Manchester, or Liverpool, by the evening Trains, are generally delivered early on the following morning.

The fact that trains could leave intermediate stations as soon as they were ready, rather than waiting until the stated departure time, must have been a very frustrating experience for some passengers!

Slade Heath Railway Bridge

According to Osbornes Guide of 1840, the iron bridge carrying the railway over the canal at Slade Heath was 'handsome and strong'. Another guidebook, Drake's, describes the line from Paradise as follows:

> A bridge here crosses it, bearing the felicitous name of 'Paradise;' happy mortals, to reach such blessed bourne! But our stay is brief indeed; Paradise is left far behind, and we pass onwards under and over many a bridge of great and small degree; for the railroad even renders a common dirty gutter, a thing of so great importance, that a stately and ponderous arch must be erected for its insignificant accommodation! The Stafford Canal passes under, and the railroad over, a handsome iron

Figure 73: Abutment on Slade Heath bridge. (Author)

bridge, between the village of Coven on the West, and Aspley on the East side of the line.

The bridge consisted of a single arch of 32 foot span, at a height of 11 feet above the water. The present-day bridge is a typical concrete affair although the tops of the abutments at least continue the pattern of the original stonework below.

Railway Accidents

As well as providing inspiration, business opportunities and employment for local residents, the railway was also the scene of numerous accidents in the area. One of the earliest, in 1845, was that which befell railway worker William Heath at Coven Heath at about 2.30 on a Friday afternoon. He was standing on the 'down' (northbound) line looking northwards at the Liverpool mail train, when he was struck from behind by the Birmingham mail. The engine driver had sounded his whistle continuously when he saw Heath on the line and a co-worker also tried to attract his attention but to no avail. Heath was killed on the spot and his body dreadfully mangled in the accident.

Given the novelty of railways at that time, it is easy to imagine how Heath had become enthralled by the Liverpool train and not given sufficient thought to the possibility of a train approaching from behind.

In the early days of the railway, employees were at least as likely as passengers and pedestrians to come to grief. One particularly common and unpleasant occurrence was contact between the head of driver, fireman, guard or passenger and an over-bridge. It may seem inconceivable today but it was not out of the ordinary for employees to clamber around and over the engine and coaches while the train was in motion. Furthermore, it was commonplace for passengers to travel on the roof of a carriage even when there were free seats within. It will be seen from the company regulations that this was not specifically prohibited, only that passengers should minimise the risk of accident by always alighting from the left-hand side of the train.

One such accident happened to the fireman of a train as it passed under a bridge near Four Ashes station, just two years after the railway opened. As there was no access to the rest of the train from the engine, fireman John Rigby climbed over the roof to ask a man in one of the carriages for some tobacco. As he was returning, his head struck the bridge and was he was killed instantly. One newspaper report described Rigby's actions as a 'dangerous indiscretion' but, being before any form of 'Health and Safety' legislation, it was, unquestionably, thought to be his own fault.

Accidents happened on every conceivable part of the railways in their formative years but as time went by, safety very gradually improved. Nevertheless, certain parts of the infrastructure continued to be accident black-spots and chief among these were tunnels, junctions and stations. Although there were a couple of minor sidings on this stretch of the railway (at Four Ashes and later at Paradise), Four Ashes Station posed the greatest risk of injury or death, especially for passengers.

In spring 1904, Agnes Maud Fox of Brewood was struck by an

express when crossing the tracks at Four Ashes. She had arrived by bicycle intending to go to Birmingham but was late for her train. As she dashed across the line she was hit by the locomotive and decapitated. Her mutilated body was found 'in the four foot' (i.e. between the tracks) and her head some distance away. To quote one newspaper, "the horrifying spectacle had a sickening influence upon the spectators".

The inquest jury recommended that the crossing between platforms be protected by a gate controlled by the signalman, or better still, that a subway be provided to avoid such accidents in future.

Ten years later there was another accident on the station level crossing, this time sixty-two-year-old Augustus Fowler of Wolverhampton was the victim. The inquest jury heard that the level crossing gate (presumably installed after the earlier accident) was not closed and that there was no footbridge between the platforms! The jury returned a verdict of accidental death.

Coven Heath resident George Cowley, who was in his mid-twenties, worked for the London & North Western Railway (as the Grand Junction had become in 1846) at Bushbury Junction. While he was attaching wagons to a train, he was knocked down by a goods train passing on an adjacent line and both his legs were severed. Despite the seriousness of his injuries, Cowley survived and was still working as a railway porter in 1891, almost a decade after the accident.

In 1898 a bizarre accident occurred near Four Ashes, when a young man seems to have jumped from a moving train in the early hours of the morning. Albert Macdonald, an eighteen-year-old sailor, had left his ship at Chatham and taken the midnight mail train from London. As the train passed Four Ashes, signalman William Evans heard a 'thump' as if something had hit his signal box and when he stepped outside, he found the body of Macdonald. Evans immediately wired ahead to Stafford to have the train stopped and examined, in the hope of determining whether the young man had fallen from the train or been knocked down by it.

Since no damage was found on the engine and there were no open carriage doors it was assumed that the man had jumped. This speculation seemed to be backed up when letters to a friend at Brewood were found on his body, although he had no money, no ticket and no luggage. He was however carrying two photographs of himself and a young woman, which had been taken at a Wolverhampton studio. The most likely explanation for his death was that he had sought a free ride on the train, on or between the coaches or guards van, and tried to dismount somewhere near the station.

In 1907, the mutilated body of another man was found on the track near Four Ashes by a railway plate-layer, but in this instance the man could not be identified. All the man's limbs had been severed from the trunk, which was cut in two, and his head completely smashed, presenting "a most revolting spectacle" according to one report.

Thankfully not all incidents on the railway were accompanied by such serious or gruesome consequences. For example, early one February morning in 1855, a partially loaded goods train from Liverpool to Birmingham had just passed Four Ashes, when two men travelling in the brake-van at the rear of the train saw the outer 'tyre' break away from a wheel on one of the wagons ahead. Following proper procedure, the men quickly screwed down the van's brakes, but the couplings on the faulty wagon broke and the train was divided.

Despite the train travelling at only 18 mph, the wagon and its neighbour were flung violently from the rails. The driver didn't realise that his 26 wagon consist had been shortened until about five minutes later, when he found that he could no longer see the lights of the brake van. As was common practice in those days, he simply reversed up the track to find out what had happened! It is interesting to note that the train had been travelling for over six and a half hours when it came to grief and would have taken another hour to reach its final destination.

In March 1875, a train known as the Birmingham Irish Mail came to grief just south of Four Ashes station. The train, which conveyed post left by the Irish Mail at Stafford onwards to Birmingham, struck an oil-filled iron tank that had fallen from an earlier goods train. The locomotive, which was travelling at full speed, was derailed and tore up a short section of track before being brought to a halt without injury to any member of the train crew.

The Albrighton Hunt met at Stretton on a spring day in 1880, and soon managed to flush a fox from the woods at Crateford. After leading the chase through Somerford Park and Standeford, the poor creature took to the line near Four Ashes, with the hounds in close pursuit, just as an express train was approaching. Fortunately the signalman was alert and, having spotted the dogs on the line, was able to bring the train to a stand before the seemingly inevitable carnage took place.

A summer thunderstorm rumbled across much of the Midlands one June day in 1893, accompanied by torrential rain. A culvert beneath the line at Coven couldn't cope with the sudden downpour and water washed across the railway, taking away a large quantity of ballast from beneath the rails. Thanks to the typical 'can do' attitude of Victorian engineers, the line was closed for less than half a day while repairs were made, allowing the all-important mail trains to run once more.[24]

Four Ashes Station

Some three decades after the Grand Junction was built, people could still wax lyrical about the juxtaposition of this modern transport system and the attractive countryside through which it ran. A regular 1867 newspaper column, about one man's countryside walks, described Four Ashes Station on a summer's evening:

> "At this diminutive roadside station, in the midst of a fair and peaceful landscape, I had an ample space to reflect on my long day's ramble. It was growing far into the twilight and the surrounding fields were white with silvery sheen. Not a sound disturbed the serene stillness, save the night winds waving the distant woods, or the tramp of the solitary traveller along the neighbouring road."

Figure 74: Pedestrians and carts heading to and from the station at Four Ashes. (M. Nicholls)

The scene is so peaceful that the author begins to imagine the area in the days of centuries gone by, but before long, a rumble in the distance indicates the approaching train, which soon draws near and dispels his fantasy.

The station went on to serve the local populace for almost a hundred years more, finally closing in 1959, but by that time it lay in a very different environment, due to the growth of the adjacent industrial estate.

The 'carbon works', producing lamp-black for use in rubber products, was established here around 1920 and the Midland Tar Distillers refinery in the middle of the century. Sidings opposite the station signal box were used by this firm and they also operated a special type of locomotive. The risk of igniting their petroleum products meant that a conventional coal-fired engine was out of the question. Instead, they used a 'rechargeable' fireless locomotive. In place of the usual boiler barrel was a simple tank that could be topped-up with steam produced in a safe area of the works.

Gailey had its own station in the cutting immediately south of Watling Street. Originally known as the 'Spread Eagle', the distance between this and Four Ashes was so short that in the days of steam it must have been time to apply the brakes almost as soon as the train got going![25]

The Railway to Brewood

Some 30 years after the age of 'railway mania', improbable rail schemes were still being hatched in many parts of the country. In 1874, The Brewood & Wolverhampton Railway Company made an application to build a branch, approximately 2 miles in length, from the LNWR's Grand Junction line to Brewood. The proposed railway would run from a junction at Slade Heath, through Standeford, Somerford and Catchem's End, and terminate in the garden of Mr Brewster on the east side of Engleton Lane.

Regardless of the economic case for this branch line, construction would have meant dealing with a number of difficult practical issues. Firstly, the junction would be on a tall embankment and would have to cross the Stafford Road almost immediately. It would also have to bridge Saredon Brook and the Penk and negotiate two more roads before reaching its terminus. On top of that it would have to pass within a few tens of yards of Somerford Hall.

Within a year the initial plan was abandoned and the Company tried a new tack, making a fresh application to branch from the main line at Fordhouses, run through Leescroft, Brinsford and Coven and on to Brewood.

This southern route would have faced similar problems to the first proposal but, depending upon the exact route, might also have had to contend with the Shropshire Union canal and parts of the Chillington estate!

Given the number of obstacles involved for such a short railway, and the uncertain financial benefits for investors, it is no surprise that the company was soon forced to abandon its plans entirely and it was wound up in 1879. We can only wonder at the impact on Coven and its surroundings if either of these schemes had come to fruition.[26]

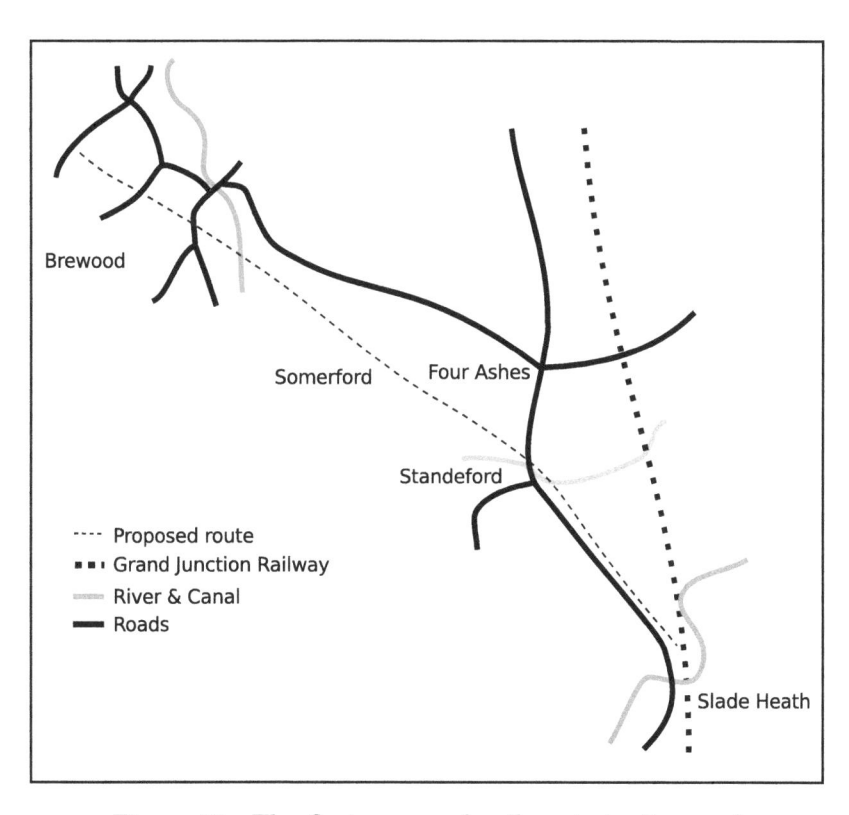

Figure 75: The first proposed rail route to Brewood.

Royal Ordnance Factory Featherstone

Despite its official title (and the LMSR railway designation of 'Bushbury Ordnance Factory'), this World War II munitions depot was located at Paradise. Contractors Bovis and Pauling began construction in December 1940 but production did not commence until the spring of 1942. In typical public sector style, the estimated cost of £2 million was considerably less than the final £3.3 million bill.

ROF Featherstone was a 'filling station', that is, it was responsible for packing cartridge and shell cases with explosive produced elsewhere. Its primary output, under the management of Courtaulds, was cartridge caps for small arms, and ammunition for the hand-held PIAT anti-tank weapon. The PIAT was a spring-loaded launcher of similar size to a rifle, with a range of around 100 yards. It was very unpopular with those who had to use it as the powerful spring mechanism meant considerable effort was required to cock the weapon and firing it would usually result in a nice bruise!

Initially the factory's rail sidings were connected to the mainline with a 'ground frame' to control train movement, but this was replaced, in 1941, by a signal box on the west side of the line. At the same time a two platform station was constructed within the sidings and adjacent to the main line, to allow workers to be brought in. It seems that the station was never used for its intended purpose as most workers either arrived by bus or lived (or were billeted) nearby.

At the end of World War II, a large number of tanks and artillery pieces, which had been stored on the western side of the dual carriageway between Coven Heath and Gailey, were loaded onto trains at Paradise to be taken elsewhere.

The factory remained on the Ministry of Defence reserve list, although not in active production, until 1952. It was deemed unsuitable for re-use because of the risk of mining subsidence. Almost no trace of the northern end of the factory is visible today, although steps and handrails that were installed on the New Road bridge can still be seen. Much of the southern part of the depot still stands, albeit in a very dilapidated state.

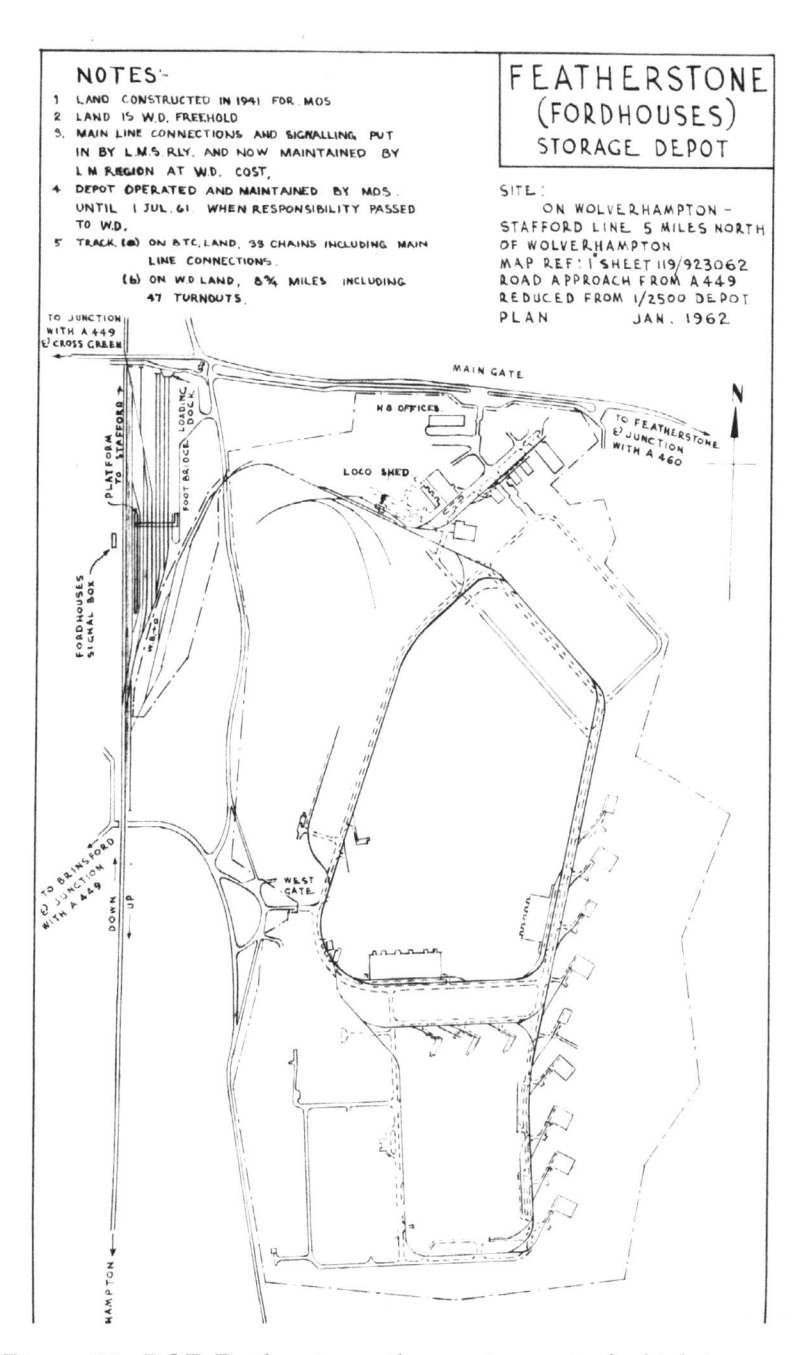

Figure 76: ROF Featherstone, the greater part of which is now covered by Featherstone Prison.

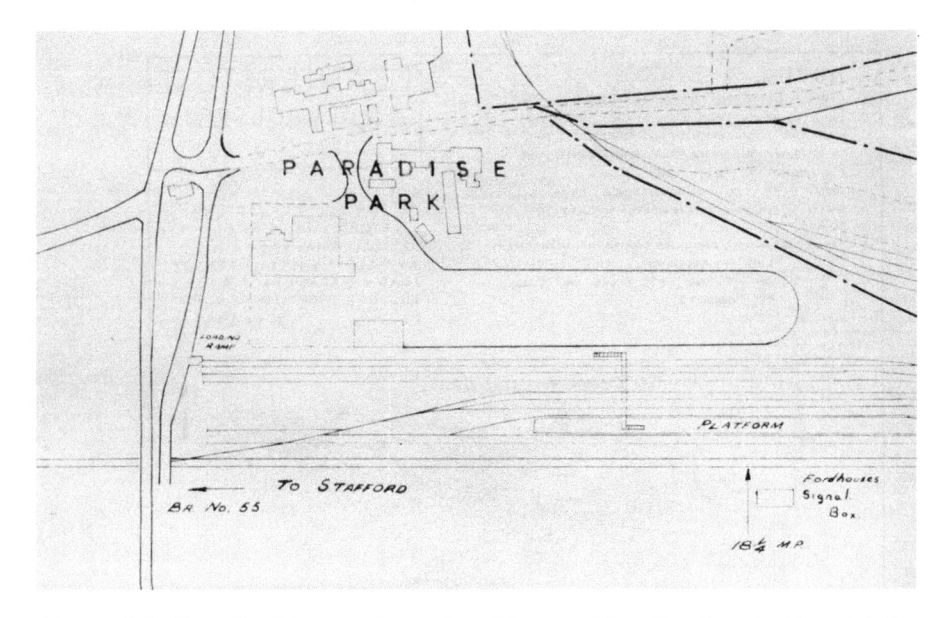

Figure 77: Detail of the station, signal box and loading bay in the vicinity of Paradise and Manor farms.

Old Roads

A map in Drakes 'Road Book of the Grand Junction Railway', published in 1838, shows the original course of the Old Stafford Road at that complicated road, rail and canal juncture at Slade Heath. The road crossed the canal in a north-easterly direction, then turned north west toward Standeford. The embanked railway running north-north-west therefore cut off a small arc of road, which now lies behind the gated underpass. This segment of land was described as waste ground belonging to the railway company when the local tithe map was drawn up around 1840. The original straight track to Aspley Farm ran from the Old Stafford Road beside what is now the waterworks. Traces of the old lane on the east side of the railway can be clearly seen in satellite and aerial photographs.

Similar straightening was applied to Paradise Lane on the east side of the railway, it originally met the lane running to The Laches

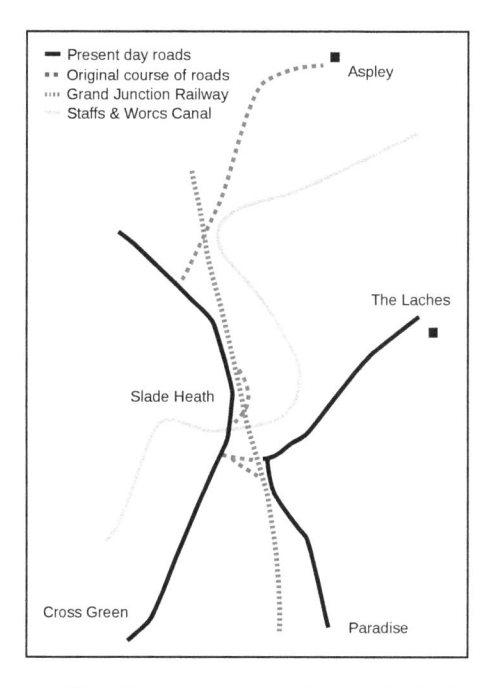

Figure 78: Changes to roads at Slade Heath.

from a south easterly direction across land that is now occupied by business premises. The bottom end of Dark Lane, which originally joined Brinsford Lane slightly further east, was likewise altered.

A track that ran parallel and very close to the canal in a north-westerly direction from Four Ashes to join Crateford Lane, was all but obliterated by the construction of the railway and the industrial estate. Even so, its path can still be discerned in the alignment of trees and a field entrance on 'Gravelly Way' and the course of the track to Marsh Farm from the A449. It continued past this point finally meeting Watling Street near Pennocrucium. This track almost certainly had its southern origin at Aspley Farm where a short stub running due north remains today.

Another lane on the south side of Station Road, roughly halfway between the railway and the canal, was known as Paddys Lane, after the farming family who lived at its end; Andrew Paddy being the farmer in the 1830s. The fields between Paddys Lane and the

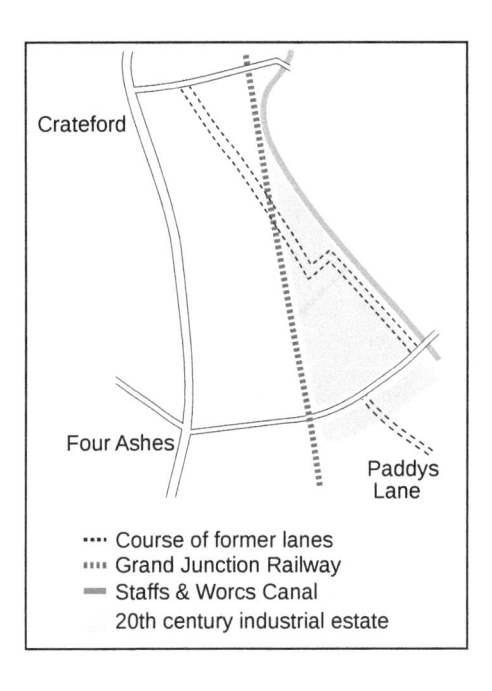

Figure 79: Former lane to Crateford.

railway were known as 'White Hay' and were farmed by Richard Bowdler, who lived opposite at that time. A tiny fragment of White Hay remains, on the west side of the railway, the site now being occupied by a bungalow.

Four Ashes Farm lay on the other side of Paddys Lane and was farmed by Edwin Kirk, son of the keeper of the Four Ashes Inn, around the end of the nineteenth century.

When farm fields are individually sold for development, subsequent building naturally tends to conform to the shape of the field. As a result, the original form of the field can often be discerned, especially from aerial or satellite photographs, even though all physical traces of hedgerows and so on may have disappeared. This trait can be seen precisely by comparing recent developments at Penkside and Birchcroft with maps from a few years ago.

Two sandstone posts beside the pavement on Poplars Farm Way mark the points where the former footpath crossed two fields, as

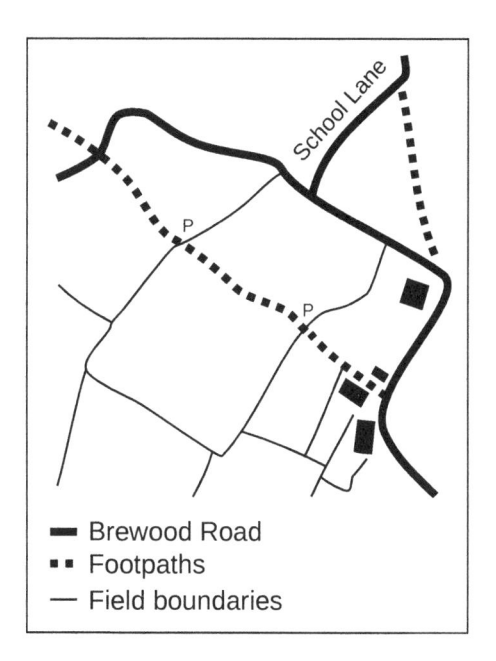

Figure 80: Footpaths and hedgerows near Poplars Farm before 1980.

indicated in the diagram. The field boundary hinted at by one of these posts remained as a track running beside the public allotments to Chambley Green until recently stopped-up. The short stub of road beside the old village bakery, which was later extended to become Poplars Farm Way, is said by some to represent an entrance to the medieval fields of the village but most of the evidence points to the opposite side of the village having the older open-field forms of agriculture.

As mentioned above, the old Stafford Road is believed to follow the course of a Roman road as it passes Coven. By the mid-1700s this road divided a little north of Standeford, with one arm heading due north to Gailey and the other in a north-westerly direction through Crateford (or Crakeford as it may once have been known) to the Roman villa at Engleton.

By the 20th century, the first segment of this latter route had fallen out of use, although its path can still be discerned in field and plantation boundaries. The point at which it began is indicated by

Figure 81: Route of former lane past Standeford Farm.

the alignment of the two buildings at Standeford Farm and woodland along its course on the north side of Four Ashes Road was known as 'Old Lane Wood'..

The track passes through Somerford wood, between Standeford and Four Ashes Road, a part of the Somerford estate known as 'Forrester's Close', which has been used for rearing pheasants since at least 1824. Incidentally, according to one newspaper report, Somerford gamekeeper Mr Richards shot a Golden Eagle near here in 1858. This must have been one of the last specimens of this majestic bird of prey in the vicinity, as the species is believed to have been extinguished in England around this time. The Somerford estate was said to have been almost completely denuded of timber by about 1800 but the Honourable Edward Monckton rectified this during the succeeding decades.

To the south of Coven, there are numerous tracks connecting Lawn Lane with the Old Stafford Road, the Old Mill at Coven Heath, the Anchor Inn and so on. All of these pathways are at

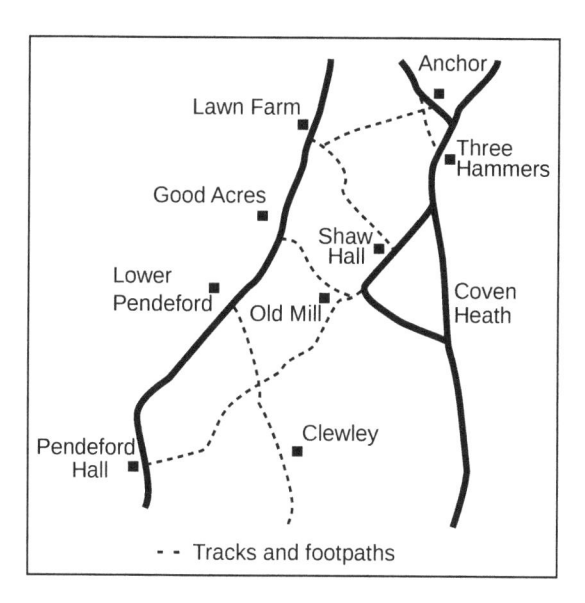

Figure 82: The network of paths connecting roads and buildings around Coven Heath.

least 250 years old, some may be considerably older; that in the vicinity of the Old Mill is said to have been used by Charles in his escape from Boscobel and it does have the appearance of an ancient hollow way in places.

The track from Lawn Farm to Shaw Hall was probably known as Shaw Lane - an adjacent field had the name Shaw Lane Leasow when the tithe map was drawn up.

Until the middle of the twentieth century, a road ran from near the crossroads at Paradise, in a south easterly direction towards Moseley Hall. The section nearest Paradise was wiped out with the construction of the Royal Ordnance Factory during World War II. The ninety degree turn on East Road, at Brinsford, marks the point where this old road joined.

Several inhabitants of Coven complained to the Parish Council about the danger of children playing on the public roads in 1896. A deputation was appointed to examine some land that Mr Copeland, of Grange Farm, had offered to rent to the council as a recreation ground. This was probably the field that actually became the recre-

Figure 83: A traction engine at work, in this case delivering one of the boilers for the new pumping station at Slade Heath. (SSW archives)

ation ground and was later developed as Green Acres; certainly the cottages there belonged to Grange Farm.

In 1908, the road between Coven and Brewood was adjudged by the Council Surveyor to have been considerably damaged by traction engine traffic; not unsurprising when one considers that a road locomotive might weight 15 tons or more. These lumbering giants were used to drive threshing equipment, to power saw mills and to move exceptional loads, mostly on farms. They were too expensive and complex for farmers to own and maintain so would be hired when needed. As a result, they travelled extensively on already poor rural lanes and sometimes came to grief crossing bridges which were built long before the age of steam began.

Members of the council must have known who owned the engines concerned, as they resolved to recover costs of a little over £3 from those responsible. There were two traction engine drivers living at Cross Green in 1911 but such engines had been used in and around the village for at least thirty years before this date.

By the 1930s roads in the area had improved considerably - for

Figure 84: The A449, looking towards Light Ash, in the 1950s.

a few decades after construction, and before the dramatic rise in car ownership, the A449 dual carriageway offered motorists a modern 'open road', as can be seen in the accompanying photographs.[27]

Waterworks

There are two water pumping stations in the vicinity of Coven, one at Somerford and a second at Slade Heath. When plans for the two stations were presented to parliament in 1915 by the South Staffordshire Waterworks company, they were opposed by Wolverhampton and Cannock councils, who feared that the stations would interfere with their water supplies, and by the Staffordshire and Worcestershire Canal Company who claimed that the pumps would reduce the flow from springs in the area which fed into the canal.

These objections, the effects of the war and increasing costs, meant that Somerford didn't open until 1923 and Slade Heath until the following year.

The test borehole at Somerford pumping station was around two

Figure 85: No traffic lights and no road markings at The Harrows.

feet in diameter and reached a depth of more than one thousand feet! The cores obtained from the boring work provided valuable geological information about the various sandstone strata in the area and the station was able to supply around 700 gallons per minute from a depth of about 200 feet.

The four boreholes at Slade Heath reached a depth of 600 feet and the works delivered over two million gallons of water every day. The boilers for the pumping engines were supplied with coal via the canal. The fuel was unloaded at the adjacent wharf and taken on a short tramway underneath the LNWR railway to the boiler house. The metal bases of unloading equipment can still be seen on the wharf, as can the tunnel beneath the railway.

Rubble from construction and drilling of the boreholes was taken by contractor's light railway alongside the main-line in a northerly direction. A temporary crossing was built, parallel to the railway bridge, over the lane to Aspley Farm, and the rubble dumped in the next field. This stony debris still lies on the surface, preventing

Figure 86: View from the south side of the waterworks during construction. (SSW archives)

a large area from being cultivated.

The station employed two triple expansion steam engines which remained in service until around 1970, when the facility was modernised. Some of the old station remains, hidden beneath the modern single storey building.[28]

Water Pumps

As well as containing harmful bacteria, water from rivers and lakes has always been prone to contamination by industrial, domestic and farm waste. As a consequence, people in the past relied upon ground water from natural springs and wells, and later, from water pumped up via bore-holes, for drinking purposes.

The sandstone underlying this area acts as a giant sponge or 'aquifer', from which water will readily flow into a bore-hole. Unlike

Figure 87: One of the station's boilers, unhitched from the traction engine to enter the site. (SSW archives)

Figure 88: The two boilers in operation. In some pumping stations it was usual to run one boiler and keep the other in reserve. A tramway coal wagon can be seen at left. (SSW archives)

Figure 89: The newly completed works. (SSW archives)

Figure 90: The triple expansion steam engine 'W W Wiggin', named after one of the directors of the company. (SSW archives)

Figure 91: Almost 100 years on and the rubble near Aspley Farm prevents this part of the field from being ploughed. The railway embankment runs along the middle of the photograph. (Author)

river water, this is usually free from contaminants and safe to drink, being effectively 'scrubbed' as it slowly circulates within the top 100 metes or so of rock. Although water can be found a mile or more below the surface, there was a practical limit of about twenty five feet for traditional, manually operated water pumps, which relied upon suction and a simple non-return valve in the pipe. These valves were comprised of leather weighted with a lead 'clack', so named after the noise they made as the valve fell back into place.

A brief survey of water pumps in the area towards the end of the Victorian era shows how shallow ground water was readily available throughout the district. The vast majority of these pumps have disappeared, although a few might remain as garden ornaments. The number of springs that could be found in the area and the continuous operation of two water pumping stations adds further testament to the availability of potable water under our feet.

There were hand operated pumps in the following locations:

In front of Forge House
Behind the cottages at the bottom of Lower Avenue and at Stone House
At the rear of the Methodist church
In the garden of the farmhouse at the bottom of Church Lane
At Coven Farm and behind the Brewood Road cottages opposite
In front of Coven House
At the rear of Birch Croft on the Brewood Road
In the yard at The Beeches
At the back of Grange Farm
In front of the cottages belonging to Grange Farm on Brewood Road near School Lane
In the garden of the cottage by Brewood Park bridge
At Brewood Park Farm
At the rear of Mount Pleasant farm
At Cinder End House at the top of Cinder Hill
At The Harrow Inn
At the rear of the Four Ashes Inn
At the rear of the cottage at Standeford Green
Behind the houses opposite Barr Farm
Beyond the mill pond at Standeford Mill
In the gardens opposite St Paul's school
Two near the end of Light Ash
At the rear of the canal-side cottage at Slade Heath and behind the Black Lion
At the rear of the cottage opposite Standeford Lodge
Five pumps between Slade Heath Bridge and Paradise cross roads
At Bridge Farm and behind the barns at Brinsford Farm
At several cottages on Shaw Hall Lane and at Shaw Hall Farm
At Paradise Farm
At Pendeford Cottage and Lower Pendeford Farm
At the rear of Lawn Farm
At the cottages off Club Lane, Coven Heath
In front of the cottages on Meadow Lane, Coven Heath

In the garden of Hordern Cottages, Coven Heath
At Old Mill Farm

In addition to these and no doubt others unrecorded, there were wells at The Rookery, Lower Green near the Penk and at Three Hammers farm.

Sewage Works

Fields around the Old Mill Farm at Coven Heath were used for sewage treatment at the start of the twentieth century. These 'sewage farms', where human waste was carted or pumped to the site and then spread on fields or evaporated in tanks, had been around for at least fifty years. Alfred Matthews, the sewage farm bailiff employed by Heath Town Urban District Council, lived on site at Old Mill Farm before the Great War - we can only assume that one would get used to the smell! The treatment plant at Coven Heath was built around 1940, although a large sewage tank is shown immediately adjacent to the canal bridge on a map of 1927.

Four sewage treatment beds were also built in Coven, on land near the confluence of Saredon Brook and the Penk at Mount Pleasant, with access to the site via the track from Standeford Green. They were only in use for a couple of decades from the late 1950s but their remains persist.

The Staffs & Worcs Canal

As far back as 1717, Thomas Congreve proposed creating a navigable waterway between Severn and Trent by improving the rivers Penk and Sow, and adding sections of man-made canal where necessary. In the event it had to wait half a century, until the building of the Staffordshire & Worcestershire was authorised by an act of Parliament in 1766. Considering that it required labour on an unprecedented scale, using nothing more than shovel, pick, dynamite and horse, its opening in 1772 testifies to the brilliance of its chief engineer James Brindley. Construction was planned in meticulous detail and included a long series of rules to deal with every aspect of the venture, including who was responsible for what, how accounts were to be kept for materials, how the workforce was to be paid, how many horse-drawn journeys were made and so forth.

The predominantly Irish workers known as 'navvies' (a contraction of 'navigators') who carried out the excavation, camped alongside the canal as work progressed and there was frequent tension between these men and those of villages along the route. In addition to the navvies, there were scores of skilled bricklayers, stonemasons, carpenters and boat-wrights.

The canal snakes through the outskirts of Coven on its fifty mile course, linking the Severn at Stourport to the Trent & Mersey Canal at Great Heywood. By following contours in the landscape construction was simplified, as fewer cuttings, embankments, tunnels and locks were required than a direct route would demand.

Like all canals, it brought huge benefits to those who lived along its length, not just to the industries that inspired its creation. While transporting raw materials such as coal, iron ore and finished goods formed the backbone of canal trade, boats also brought coal for domestic use, fertiliser for farms and slate for the roofs of houses. Compared to road transport of the time, the canal was quicker, safer for fragile cargo and able to handle much greater loads.

Once the canal was open, pathways soon sprang up to provide the shortest possible routes to and from the village. In addition to the Brewood Road linking Coven to the canal at Cross green, footpaths took a direct easterly route from Church Lane down to the canal and in a south easterly direction to the Anchor.

The coming of rail transport heralded the decline of the canal system but dwindling traffic continued up until the nationalisation of all canals, shortly after the second World War. On the night of Sunday 7th April 1861, at a time when railways were still burgeoning, there were six working boats moored at Coven, some occupied by a boatman and his assistant, others by entire families. It seems likely that there would have been many more boats berthed there on a comparable night half a century before, in addition to the 'day boats' that plied back and forth on shorter journeys.

Boatmen were not the only people to live and work in a form of 'mobile home'; at the 1851 census there were three groups of people living in their carts beside the turnpike road at Coven Heath. One cart was occupied by Joseph Smith along with his wife and baby daughter, and the other two by single men. All three men were hardware traders and each had a 13 or 14 year-old servant with them.

Ball Lane Canal Bridge

Although quite narrow today, the bridge at Coven Heath was originally much smaller, as can be seen from the line of the arch on the northern side. Of the two dwellings known as Hordern Cottages, that nearest the canal was a popular tea-room in the first decade of the twentieth century, with its own landing stage. This was despite the fact that fields just across the bridge were being spread with sewage!

The bridge has been extensively repaired over the last two centuries and is now in a dilapidated state with crumbling mortar, broken and missing brickwork and several redundant and decaying pieces of pipework.

Stafford Road Bridge, Cross Green

The bridge at Cross Green carries a benchmark from the original Ordnance Survey levelling project. The mark has a metal bolt embedded at the junction of the lines.

Nearby Dark Lane may have acquired its name because the bordering hedges were rarely cut back - the road was therefore very narrow and dark.

Stafford Road Bridge, Slade Heath

The accompanying photograph shows brick pillars and a beam, carrying the water main from the newly built pumping station. The

Figure 92: Hordern Cottages beside the bridge at Ball Lane.

Figure 93: Ball Lane bridge today. (Author)

Figure 94: Recent photograph of Cross Green bridge with benchmark inset. (Author)

narrowboat beyond is loaded with bricks. Walter Aston, a farmer, lived at the canal-side cottage and wharf in the 1830s.

There were numerous complaints about the three bridges carrying the Stafford Road over the Staffordshire & Worcestershire canal in the early 1800s. These 'humpback' bridges at Brinsford, Cross Green and Slade Heath were typical of those that the company were compelled to build before the canal opened in 1772.

At the time of construction they would have been adequate for foot, horse and farm traffic but with the coming of mail coaches a decade or so later, and the general increase in commercial transport over the following decades, the bridges were found to be inadequate and dangerous, especially as the entire Stafford Road was notoriously narrow to begin with.

The northern approach to the bridge at Slade Heath, and the southern approach to that at Cross Green, were described as so steep that one carriage could not see another approaching until it was too late. Although the bridge at Brinsford was demolished when the Stafford Road was improved, the other two remain and each still has a steep ascent on one side (although that at Slade Heath was reduced after being re-routed when the railway was constructed).

The original bridge at Slade Heath was roughly half its present width and until recently had a benchmark with a hole to accommodate a 3/4" steel ball used in the surveying process. The wall was demolished around 2012. The nearby 'winding hole', for turning canal boats, is not shown on maps until about 1900.

Photographs of the construction of the waterworks wharf, a little further north, show dozens of bricklayers at work at the same time - closing the canal was a costly business and work would need to be completed as quickly as possible.[29]

Stafford Road Bridge, Brinsford

The approaches to this bridge, carrying the Stafford Road over the canal near Brinsford, were less steep than others in the area and the parapet was completely flat. A 1907 photograph shows an idyllic

Figure 95: Slade Heath bridge in January 1923. The lower course of bricks (now removed) shows how little headroom was available to boats. (SSW archives)

Figure 96: Slade Heath bridge with benchmark (inset). The wall was demolished around 2012. (Author)

Figure 97: Construction of the canal wharf, during which a section of the canal was drained almost completely. (SSW archives)

scene with a fisherman on the tow-path and Coven Heath Wood beyond.

The Shropshire Union Canal

Coven is bounded on the opposite side by the Shropshire Union Canal, which leaves the Staffordshire & Worcestershire at Autherley Junction, Pendeford, skirts the western edge of Brewood Park Farm and runs onward for some sixty miles to Ellesmere Port. The canal has a rural aspect for most of its length and although it was not completed until 1835 - more than fifty years after the Staffordshire & Worcestershire - it was for a time a very profitable venture.

There was a wharf at Bilbrook near Pendeford Mill and there are typical bridges at Pendeford Hall Lane, near The Hattons and at Port Lane but the most interesting is 'Avenue Bridge' on the wooded approach to Chillington Hall from Brewood Road. Built around 1830 by Thomas Telford, the bridge has curved parapets

Figure 98: Stafford Road bridge, Brinsford. The approaches were less steep than others in the area and the deck itself was almost flat. This 1907 photograph shows an idyllic scene with a fisherman on the tow-path and Coven Heath Wood beyond.

Figure 99: Avenue bridge features on many old postcards, this example being typical. (Author's collection)

with ornate balustrades and supporting stonework that wouldn't look out of place on the portal of a Victorian railway tunnel.

There was a wharf near Hunting Bridge, within Brewood Park Farm, where night-soil was unloaded from canal barges to be spread on the adjacent fields.

The River Penk

Pendeford Cottage Bridge

This twin-span bridge carries the track from The Hattons across the Penk to the former Lower Pendeford farm on Lawn Lane.

There have been substantial changes to the waterways in this area over the years, with various streams, including that from the mill which once stood nearby, feeding into the river both north and south of the bridge.

Until the nineteenth century, the road from Pendeford Hall towards Coven forked a little south of here, with one arm being Coven Lawn and the other being the course of the ancient Roman road. The mill and cottage lay just off the latter. The Roman road ran

Figure 100: Pendeford Cottage bridge in 2010. (Author)

across Brewood Park Farm, exiting along what is now the driveway to Brewood Road, then continuing across Somerford to join another road near Engleton Villa.

A map of 1875, detailing the Penk west of Lawn Lane, shows a curved water-course running roughly parallel to the river. This was probably a stream associated with the mill which once operated here. Pendeford Cottage also stood beside this stream, the course of which is now marked by a hedgerow. The mill reservoir may have been what is now known as 'Island Pool'. There was a stream running northwards from one of Pendeford Hall's pools to this feature until the 1940s.

The aforementioned 1875 map was drawn up to accompany a claim against Wolverhampton Corporation, in respect of their recently opened sewage works at Barnfield - landowners between Pendeford and Coven including Fowler, Monckton, Chambley and others, were all claiming compensation for an overflow of sewage onto their fields. There have been other such pollution incidents in the century or more since.

The fishing pool to the west of Pendeford Cottage bridge is a comparatively recent feature. The marsh to the south west of the bridge seems less extensive today than its appearance on some nineteenth century maps would indicate.

A brook which emanates at Essington, passes through Featherstone and Brinsford then flows under the Stafford Road is named as 'Three Hammers Brook' on a map of 1770 but is called 'Brinsford Brook' in the book by Hicks Smith. It joins Watershed Brook near to Lawn Lane, which it soon passes under, and flows into the Penk at the 'Bront'. The large field sloping down from Lawn Farm to Watershed Brook, at the south end of the Bront, was originally divided into four parts, those nearest the brook being known as 'Farther Adder Holes'.

Watershed Brook itself illustrates the way in which running water was thoroughly exploited in the past. Within a short distance it powered a mill near Moseley Old Hall, a mill at Fordhouses and the Old Mill at Coven Heath before joining the Penk, which itself had driven the two mills at Pendeford, just upstream. The combined flow then provided power to the Forge at Coven and another mill at Somerford! It is easy to see why there were sometimes disputes over the use of these waterways, when those downstream were at the mercy of those higher up if they decided to divert the flow or control it to top-up their reserves.

A second tributary to the Penk issues at Laches Lane, Slade Heath. This stream crosses the old and new Stafford roads, passes beside the school and drains into the Penk at the northern end of the Bront. This marshy, willow-filled area was described as a 'plantation' in the early 1800s.

The tall hedgerow on the west side of the Penk at the Bront, indicates the former course of a man-made waterway which flowed across Brewood Park Farm to supply the forge (later the mill) pools near the bottom of Lower Avenue. There may have been a sluice gate opposite the Bront to control the flow and divert water back into the river when it was in spate.

A small stream flowed from a spring into the marshy area at

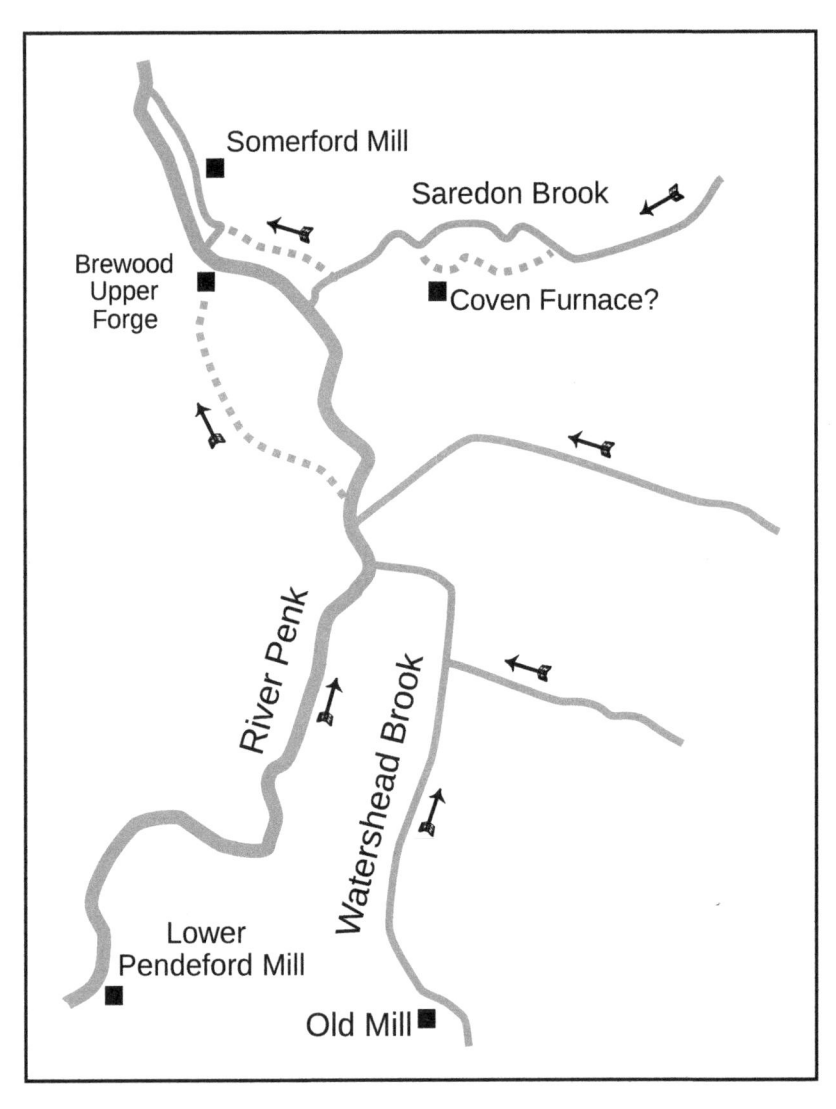

Figure 101: Tributaries to the Penk and streams to iron works and mills.

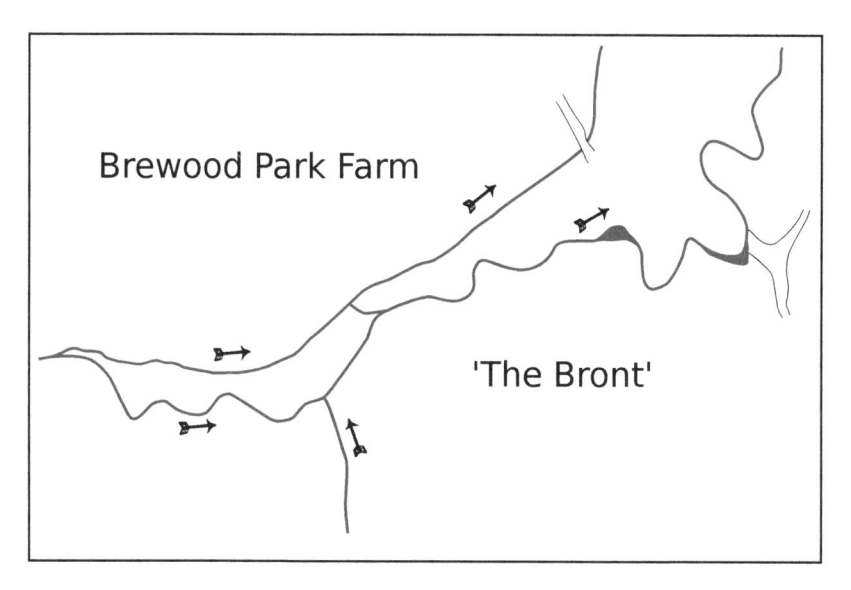

Figure 102: River Penk at The Bront, redrawn from a map of 1875. A small section of the Brewood Road can be seen at the far right.

the north end of the Bront until the mid 20th century. Its course can still be discerned along the bottom of a low bank, running through the trees beside the woodland path. There were several other natural springs in the village up until the latter third of the 20th century.[30]

The origin of the name 'Bront' is unclear; some claim it is a recent appellation, others that is ancient. The fields across which it lies were known as 'Badgers Meadow', 'The Rough Meadow' and 'Millett Field' from the 1840s or earlier.

Brewood Park Farm Bridge

At the western end of Poplars Farm Way stands a bridge over the Penk which at one time carried a track to Brewood Park Farm. This route from Lower Green seems to have come into use at some time after 1840, as there is no hint of a track or the bridge on the tithe map but it is shown on a map of the 1870s.

The track was stopped-up in the 1970s and the bridge is now

Figure 103: Bridge over the Penk at Brewood Park Farm. (Author)

in a very dilapidated condition, most of the parapet having fallen away.

Jackson's Bridge

Originally known as King's Bridge, at some time between 1834 and 1851 it became known as Jackson's Bridge, after a man who is said to have drowned (or hung himself) there. A shepherd, Charles Jackson, lived nearby in 1901 but whether he was in any way related to the man who died there is not known.

The present bridge was constructed in 1824 but it may be on the site of the ancient 'bridge of Coven, near the Park of Brewood' mentioned as far back as 1286!

There are a number of interesting marks cut into the stone above and below the bridge. Those below include a 'pointed-spade' shape and an 'XX' mark, both of which are types of mark that occur in other places in England.

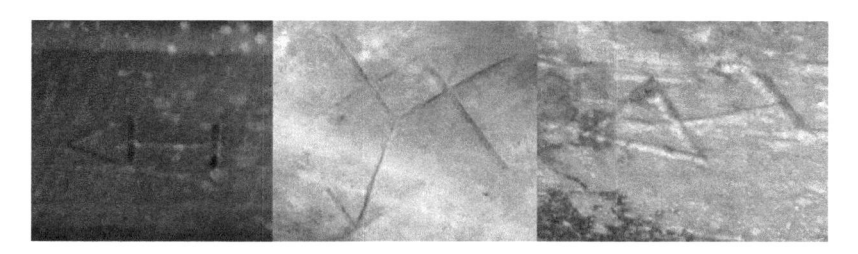

Figure 104: Stonemason's marks beneath Jackson's Bridge. (Author)

Figure 105: Very worn benchmark (inset) on Jackson's Bridge. (Author)

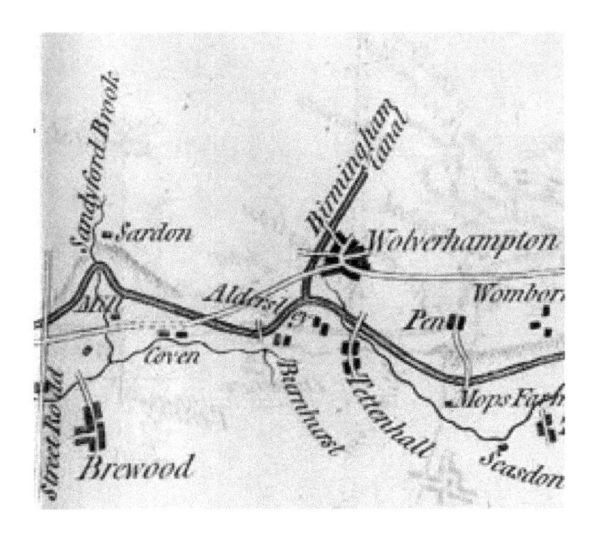

Figure 106: 'Sandyford Brook' on a map of 1771

Saredon Brook

As already mentioned, altering or regulating a water course could dramatically affect the livelihood of those downstream and there is one such case recorded as far back as 1337 regarding Saredon Brook. The miller at Standeford was accused by the Bishop of Lichfield of impeding the flow, which interfered with the operation of his mill at Somerford. The supply to this latter mill seems to have been taken off Saredon Brook immediately before it joins the Penk.

A map of the nascent Staffordshire & Worcestershire canal, published in the Gentleman's Magazine in 1771, labels the stream running to Standeford Mill as 'Sandyford' rather than 'Saredon Brook'. Standeford itself is recorded as a 'vill', i.e. a manor or parish, in the 1600s but as noted above, there was a mill here at least three hundred years before that time.

In 'A Topographical History of Staffordshire', written in 1816, the Saredon Brook was said to "abound with excellent trout" and The Harrow certainly took advantage of this, offering fishing from land at the rear of the pub.

After passing The Harrows the brook skirts woodland at Somerford, before joining the Penk near Mount Pleasant. Coven Furnace is believed to have operated in this area in the 1600s, on the south side of the brook. A small pool in this field is probably the position of the reservoir of water used to power the furnace's bellows - traces of the supply stream are visible in aerial and satellite photographs - and a small field here was known as Cinder Hill Meadow around 1840.[31]

Stafford Road Bridge, Standeford

Like many bridges of the eighteenth century and earlier, that at Standeford was very narrow. When conditions were right, it was therefore much easier for vehicles to use the adjacent ford rather than contend with other foot or horse traffic or the structure of the bridge itself!

A report dated 17th January 1799, detailed repairs required to various bridges in Staffordshire, including that at Standeford. The relevant section reads as follows:

> Standiford, the whole of the district wants gravelling and the Water in time of Floods overflows the Road so as to make it very dangerous for Travellers, this would be made quite safe, if a Culvit at each end of the Bridge was turn'd across the Road; some few Stones in the Battlements are displaced and the whole of the Railing is intirely gone away.

This damage was no doubt in part due to vehicles colliding with the parapet walls when the water was too deep to ford, but it seems that little if anything was done in response to this report. Almost a quarter of a century later, in a letter addressed to the Chairman and Magistrates at Stafford Epiphany Sessions, dated 15th January 1823, no less than nine signatories petitioned for improvements to the bridge:

> Gentlemen, We the undersigned Commissioners of the Turnpike Road leading from Wolverhampton to Stafford beg leave most respectfully to represent to you that

the old County Bridge at Standeford in the parish of Brewood over the river pink in this country is out of repair; - That it contains in length about forty yards and in breadth only eleven feet. In low water the road through the river is good, but in the Winter and after much rain the Ford through the river is not passable. And on account of the Mail Coaches and Night Coaches and other travellers going over the said Bridge Accidents have happened and the Bridge in its present state is dangerous especially so on account of the parapet walls; We therefore beg your attention to the improvement of this Bridge and that you will give such directions as you may think expedient for the safety of the Community at large.

The surveyor of the Turnpike Roads will wait on you in court to elucidate any question you may require.

The bridge of course crosses Saredon Brook rather than the Penk although the spelling 'Pink' also crops up in early surnames of the area. A note added to the letter by Mr Mander, most likely one of the magistrates, asks:

> Would not a new bridge nearly in the direction of the present ford be preferable?

The accompanying photograph was taken about a dozen years before the current bridge was built, when the dual carriageway was laid across it in the 1930s. As can be seen, it was a substantial five-span structure of solid stone with a gently curved deck. Nearly eighty years since its destruction, some of the stones can still be seen lying in the brook on the eastern side.

Figure 107: Standeford Bridge photographed in March 1923. (SSW archives)

Chapter 4
People, Occupations and Pastimes

Coven At The 1881 Census

The population census, taken every ten years since 1841 except during the Second World War, provides a wealth of interesting detail about individuals and their families. People were required by law to provide truthful information about their name, age and place of birth, as well as their occupation and marital status. Comparing census details with other records shows that the vast majority of people complied with this obligation, even though some took liberties with their age and marital condition or the legitimacy of their children!

Coven would have been much quieter by day and much darker by night when the 1881 census was taken. There was no motor car, aeroplane, radio or television, and an electrical supply to the village was still several decades in the future. With the exception of passing trains and an occasional steam-powered agricultural engine, the loudest sounds would have been the clatter of horse and cart in street and field, the sound of pigs and chickens, which were kept by almost every household, and the occasional sound of a piano or accordion. The narrowboat and penny-farthing added a whisper to the sound-scape in the same way that the paraffin lamp and candle bestowed almost nothing upon the night.

Twenty years earlier, when lock-making was more conspicuous in the village, the streets had their own form of background 'music', as the Birmingham Daily Gazette reported when discussing Willenhall, Brewood and Coven:

> Diverse little lock-shops are scattered throughout the parish, in which one may hear the tapping of innumerable hammers in monotonous chorus, relieved at intervals by the shriller melody of a file.

Houses were warmed by coal fires, sometimes in more than one room. On the coldest winter night a bucket of burning coal may have been taken to a bedroom, if there was no fireplace, despite the risk of fire and carbon monoxide poisoning. Other than this, the warmth of the chimney breast or maybe a bedpan or oven-heated brick wrapped in a cloth were the only comfort.

Although this was the era of great municipal projects to provide clean running water and refuse and sewage disposal, small villages such as Coven would not have these luxuries until very much later. Nevertheless, the underlying geology of the locality ensured that fresh water was always available to be pumped up by hand and every household had its own privy, the contents of which would be carted away to be spread on fields as 'night-soil'. Many cottages would also have a 'midden', a spot in the garden to deposit household waste. Although some refuse such as old furniture or clothes could be burned, there was no other means of disposing of bottles, bones and metallic items.

Livestock kept at home and on farms also generated a large amount of waste. While this could be ploughed back into fields and gardens as fertiliser, it was not possible to thoroughly clean the areas in which it might accumulate. This inability to properly dispose of human and animal waste meant that water supplies were sometimes contaminated and could pose a grave risk to health. The parish council enacted and enforced by-laws to control these risks and other nuisances such as noxious trades, slaughterhouses and smoking chimneys.

It is against this backdrop then, that we take a look at just a few Coven households. The name, age, place of birth and occupation is shown for each individual but relationships and marital status have been omitted. Some of the individuals are discussed in greater detail a little later in this chapter.

Grange Farm

Thomas Clift	54	Gailey	Farmer 80 Acres
Ann Clift	60	Upstone, Staffs	Farmer's Wife
Frederick J Gripton	5	Shareshill	Scholar
Harry Pool	12	Coven	Farm Servant (Indoor)

Although the Elementary Education Act came into force a decade before this census, many adults were still barely able to read or write; if the information they supplied was unclear it would need to be checked in person by the census 'enumerator' - the official appointed to collect and collate the information. As there is no place by the name of 'Upstone' in Staffordshire, it's quite possible that Ann Clift's birthplace was given verbally as "up Stone", although it could be a badly written 'Ipstones' (in north Staffordshire). Thomas Clifft was farming here in the 1840s and, before him, James Cliffe. Despite variations in spelling these were almost certainly Thomas's father and grandfather.

Church Alley

| Mary A. Hayward | 67 | Calf Heath | Laundress |
| Elizabeth Hayward | 31 | Coven | Formerly Cook (Dom) |

There is no precise indication of where this dwelling was, although a building stood about half way along the alley on the south side until at least 1923. It has been suggested that this alleyway was at one time known as Pinfold Lane. Many villages had a pound or pinfold in which stray livestock could be held until reclaimed by the rightful owner. Coven's was almost certainly within 'Pinfold Croft' mentioned in a 'Survey of the Manor of Coven', dating from the end of the eighteenth century, and in the tithe map awards. A small

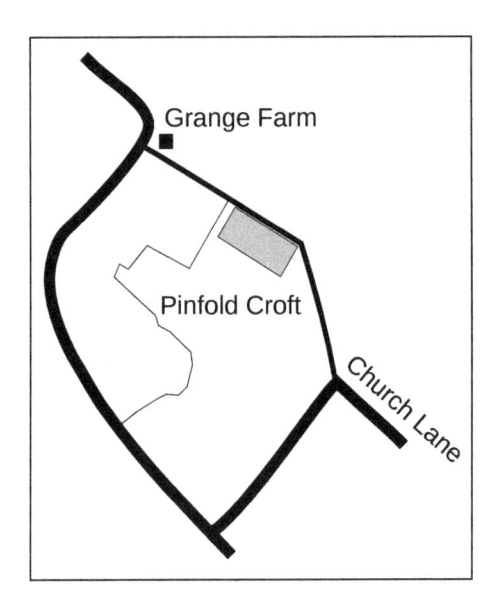

Figure 108: Probable position of Coven's pinfold, beside Pinfold Lane/Church Alley

rectangular area within Pinfold Croft is marked but unnumbered on the tithe map. Pinfold Croft itself was a large field bounded by the Brewood Road, Church Lane and this alley.

Mary Hayward was still taking in washing at the age of 67 (not an uncommon state of affairs) while her unmarried daughter was an out-of-work domestic cook.

The Rainbow

Joseph Jackson	37	Bilston	Licensed Victualler
Jane Jackson	36	Bilston	Licensed Victualler's Wife
Mary Divive	20	Wolverhampton	Servant
William Wood	50	Burton	Ostler

In the late 1800s there were many former 'beer-house keepers' who had lost their livelihood when it became necessary to obtain a license to sell spirits. As a result, people looking to stay in the trade would often move from place to place to find suitable premises. Joseph and Jane Jackson originally came from Bilston and William

Wood, the 'ostler' who looked after horses at the inn, was born at Burton upon Trent.

Poplars Farm

William R. Hughes	31	Brewood	Farmer Of 40 Acres
Elizabeth Hughes	22	Under Haywood	Housekeeper
Thomas Hughes	28	Brewood	Grocer Unemployed

This farmhouse, now Poplars Farm Cottage, stands at the end of present-day 'Poplars Farm Way'. Although there are no Poplar trees in that area now, there were two rows on land to the south of Watershead Brook opposite the 'Bront' until the 1990s and there are others where Lawn Lane enters the village.

The situation in this household is a little confusing as we have two brothers, each listed as a son, with the elder designated the head of the household but no father present. It may be that their father owned or leased Poplars Farm but lived elsewhere or was temporarily absent. Their housekeeper Elizabeth may be related or just happen to have the same name.

The New Inn

Thomas F. Hill	40	Bednall	Inn Keeper
Harriet Hill	43	Compton	
Albert W. Hill	11	Swindown, Staffs	Scholar
Thomas E. Hill	10	Pattingham	Scholar
Horace J. Hill	8	Pattingham	Scholar
Agnes Lewis	15	Brewood	Domestic Servant

The New Inn was housed in the large white-painted building on Poplars Farm Way, next to 'The Homage'. Today this building is purely residential but it has served as a pub and various types of shop in the past. The birthplaces of the Hill children show how the family had moved around various Staffordshire villages, perhaps pursuing the same trade.

Lawn Farm

Brooke Chambley	50	Coven	Farmer 350 Acres
Sarah A. Chambley	40	Edgbaston	Farmers Wife
Martha Wood	21	Wyrley	Servant Domestic

The Chambleys were farming in Coven throughout the 1800s - more information about them can be found later in this chapter.

The Vicarage

Inglis G. Monckton	49	India	Vicar Of Coven
Georgiana E. Monckton	21	Coven	
William L. Monckton	15	Coven	Scholar
Elizabeth Robinson	26	Highley, Shropshire	Housemaid
Mary E. Williams	29	Bridgnorth	Maid
Mary E. Robinson	24	Highley, Shropshire	Cook

Inglis Monckton, born in India and a member of the local landowning family, was the incumbent. All three servants, two probably being sisters, came from the Bridgnorth area.

Old School House

Edward Hodges	26	Broadway	Teacher
Eliza A. E. Hodges	29	Knightwick	Housekeeper
Kate M. Hodges	24	Droitwich	Assistant Teacher
Annie S. Hodges	15	Wickenford	Scholar
John S. Hodges	10	Wickenford	Scholar
Mary E. Taylor	15	Coven	Servant (Domestic)
Annie Nickson	7	Wales	Scholar

The old school house on Light Ash was occupied by the unmarried schoolmaster Edward Hodges and his younger brothers and sisters along with a locally born domestic servant and a 7-year-old boarder from Wales.

The Beeches

Thomas Hall	41	Cannock	Thrashing Machine Prop
Agnes Hall	41	Wolv'ton	
Agnes Hall	13	Shifnal	Scholar
Mary J Hall	10	Shifnal	Scholar
Isabel M. Hall	8	Shifnal	Scholar
Thomas F Hall	6	Shifnal	Scholar
Olive S. Hall	5	Shifnal	Scholarz
Evelyn E. Hall	3	Brewood	Scholar
Edith H. Hall	3	Brewood	Scholar
Philip H. N. Hall	10 mo.	Brewood	
Francis N. Seyde	39	Wolv'ton	Varnish Maker
Eleanor Bennett	18	Notts	Governess
John Holloway	28	Stourbridge	Machinist
Ann Bennett	16	Wednesfield	Nurse

This substantial Georgian house at the centre of the village had no less than fourteen occupants at the 1881 census, consisting of Thomas Hall and his large family, his brother in law, a visitor, a governess and children's nurse.

Hall is shown as a thrashing (i.e. threshing) machine proprietor; perhaps resident machinist John Holloway maintained or operated the engine when it was hired out to local farms.

In addition to the details censuses provide about individuals, they can be summarised to obtain additional interesting information...

> There were 274 residents (including those at Light Ash) of which 127 were male and 147 female. In 1851 the population was put at over 600 but this probably included those in the surrounding hamlets.

> There were 63 dwellings and 17 uninhabited buildings in Coven itself, giving an average of 4.3 people per household.

> The oldest villager was Thomas Wootton, a retired farm labourer, aged 81, and the youngest was Anne Shenton, born just 3 weeks before the census was taken.

Most people were born in the nearby villages of Staffordshire and Shropshire but there were also 2 people from London, 1 each from Lincolnshire, Monmouth and Dorset, a married couple from Ireland and a young Scotsman working as a blacksmith.

There were 57 schoolchildren in the village at the time of the census, representing about 20% of the total population.

More people (about 20) were employed in agriculture than in any other single occupation although 15 people are listed as servants of one kind or another. There were six farmers, three carpenters, three blacksmiths, two gardeners and two grooms within the village itself.

Miscellaneous occupations include 2 sock-makers, a varnish maker, a hawker, a coachman and a boot-maker.

As previously mentioned, lock-making was strong in Coven in the first half of the nineteenth century with many locksmiths residing in the centre of the village, at Lower Green, Light Ash, Standeford, Brinsford and Paradise, but only two people were involved in the trade by 1881; more lock-makers lived at Coven Heath however. The lock-makers of Coven specialised in making plate-locks, i.e locks to be embedded in doors, and were part of a co-operative based in Wolverhampton although they worked at home.

The commonest forenames for males in the village were...

   Thomas (22)
   John (17)
   Joseph (14)
   William (12)
   George (11)

and for females...

   Mary (27)
   Sarah (17)

Elizabeth (10)

There were more varieties of female names than male names but of the few unusual names present, all belong to males...

Brooke
Ezra
Cornelius
Inglis
Felix

The Chambleys

William Chambley was born at the very start of the nineteenth century and became a successful farmer, property owner and investor. His mother and father, Althea and Manoah were married at Penkridge, but seem to have lived in Coven throughout their married life; Manoah living at Coven Lawn after he was widowed until the time of his death in 1854. Father and son were shareholders in the Wolverhampton & Staffordshire Banking Company in 1847. The bank operated at Queen Square in Wolverhampton in its later years and finally became part of Barclays.

William, his wife Sarah and their sons, Brooke and George, occupied the Croft and farmed the surrounding fields in the 1840s, although the farm was part of the Monckton estate. A number of infants with the name Chambley, almost certainly William's children, were buried at Brewood during the 1830s.

Like many farmers William and Brooke Chambley were shooting enthusiasts. Both purchased General Game Certificates in 1856, at cost of over £4 each, which allowed them to take or shoot game on their own land or elsewhere providing they observed the laws relating to trespass.

William Chambley was clearly a leading figure at St Paul's church; at a meeting to discuss seating arrangements for the newly built church in 1857, he proposed a stained glass window for the east end. The wealth of those present meant that subscriptions entered into on the day were sufficient to cover the projected cost.

William and his family owned and lived at The Beeches in 1861 and he is known to have owned the land attached to Poplars Farm in the early '70s. He died in June 1876.

Brooke Chambley must have been a keen sportsman as, in addition to rough shooting, he was also a racehorse owner, jockey and cricketer. At the autumn meeting of the Brewood Races in 1859, he acted as one of two stewards, as well as riding his own horse 'Legs and Wings' to victory in the 'Farmer's Plate', a mile-and-three-quarter race over six fences. The race consisted of two heats and 'Legs and Wings' won both, although the first was run at a very slow pace and in the second he was able to walk over the line, the only other runner being pulled up! The prize was a sovereign and a silver cup. No doubt Mr Chambley was delighted but the event, held in conjunction with the Brewood Fair, seems to have been rather a damp squib, as one newspaper reported:

> Brewood Autumn Meeting came off yesterday. It was also Brewood fair; but that was a peculiarly dull affair, consisting of a shooting gallery, a few dismal gingerbread stalls, the man-monkey Joss and the happy family, all squeezed into a small quadrangle, or rather triangle, with quite a Scotch Sunday air.

The mood was probably not enhanced by the dull and drizzly weather although it cleared in the afternoon. The 'going' was said to be extremely heavy.

At the annual 'Wolverhampton and Brewood Steeplechase' in April 1861, Brooke rode his horse 'Miss Patty' into third position. The meeting, held near Hockerhill Farm, consisted mostly of men and horses of the Albrighton Hunt - prize-money for the race was five sovereigns with an extra twenty-five for horses of the Hunt.

Brooke Chambley married Sarah Thurstons in 1866 and together they worked a large acreage at Lawn Farm, employing 10 individuals. Nevertheless, he still found time to indulge his love of horses, showing them at many events, his small pony 'Billy', for example, was highly commended at a horse and hounds show in the summer of 1867.

In July 1872 he played alongside Frederick Keeling, of Brewood Park Farm, for Brewood cricket club. In one match the pair made an excellent stand against Penkridge and were still 'in' when the game had to be abandoned because of a violent thunderstorm.

By 1884 Brooke and his family had moved from Lawn Farm to The Beeches; presumably the house had remained in Chambley hands while occupied by Mr Hall and family in the intervening period. Around this time, Brooke Chambley, now in his 50s, along with other local notables Pullen, Oleranshaw, Clifft and Keeling, performed civic duties as elected Guardians for Penkridge Workhouse, part of the Cannock Union.

At one meeting of the Board of Guardians under the chairmanship of Lord Hatherton, Mr Hoskins, a Coven labourer, came to discuss maintenance payments for his child. Hoskins' wife was a very violent individual who had previously spent time at the Workhouse with their child but refused to remain there. The last time she left she took the child to Bishops Wood, threw it over a hedge and left it there. As this was the second time she had deserted the child it was decided to admit the infant provided that Mr Hoskins paid two shillings and sixpence per week for its upkeep.

Mrs Chambley also had interests beyond the home; in the late '80s and early '90s, she submitted a number of stories to national literary competitions, receiving prizes on several occasions. Little Ethel Oakley submitted some very short pieces to a syndicated newspaper column known as 'Childrens Hour', from about 1890, and one of these, written when she was just nine, earned her a prize. Ethel was the daughter of Richard Oakley of The Laches but perhaps she had been schooled by Mrs Chambley as her address was given as The Beeches.

Mr and Mrs Chambley passed away in the summer of 1902 but the family name lives on at Chambley Green, the small housing development opposite the Memorial Hall.[32]

Edward Adveno Brooke

Edward Brooke was a notable landscape artist, born at Stoke on Trent in 1822, who lived for a while at Standeford Cottage. He was working as an artist by the age of nineteen, when his family lived at Burslem, but by 1851 they had moved to Coven. The family consisted of Edward, his brother William, sister Elizabeth and their mother, also Elizabeth. They seem to have been a talented family; William was an engineer, mathematician and designer, and young Elizabeth a school teacher. Edward's mother, who had been a widow for at least ten years, died soon after they moved to Coven.

Edward married Mary Ann Pegg in Lancashire in 1854 and within a few years had moved to London, where he seems to have spent the rest of his life.

His book 'The Gardens of England', published in 1858, was dedicated to the Duchess of Sutherland, of Trentham Hall, and sponsored by the Duchess and other members of the nobility. In it he describes the gardens of several grand houses in the Midlands, such as the halls at Trentham, Alton, Teddesley and Enville as well as more distant stately homes.

Presumably he was studying these halls while living in Standeford, as according to the book's Preface:

> It is the result of years of labour, and, it is almost needless to add, has been completed at no small trouble and expense... The preparation of the original drawings required that the artist should be upon the spot whenever it was desirable to proceed and this not for a mere casual visit or a hurried sketch, but for the purpose of patient and careful labour. Thus, Mr Brooke has spent several summers in undivided attention to the views contained in this volume. Not satisfied with first or second studies, he has made repeated visits to each locality, and is enabled, therefore, to offer drawings which are correct and faithful in all their details.

In addition to the book, a few of his works can be seen at

Kensington Central Library and several other landscapes are widely available as reprints. He died in London in 1910 at the age of 88.[33]

John Smith And Son

John Smith, born in Coven around 1800, was a farmer, lock-maker, engineer, part-time Methodist preacher and village land-owner. His son, also John, born about 1827, became a builder of steam-powered engines for road, rail and agricultural use.

John senior was a preacher on the Wolverhampton circuit and in his late teens was listed as a trustee at the Noah's Ark Chapel in Wolverhampton. It was at his suggestion that services began in Coven. These were held on his premises until money could be raised to erect the Methodist chapel. His small home and workshop had only one bedroom which the family would give up whenever a fellow preacher came to visit.

Father and son were involved in the design and manufacture of machinery for drying and lifting grain and in 1850 Smith senior was a manufacturer of 'Rivington's patent mills'. In January 1858 John junior, who was then just over 20 years of age, demonstrated the power of one of his portable steam engines (similar to a traction engine) to a group of local gentlemen at Lawn Lane. The engine pulled out a strong hawthorn hedge, roots and all, in eight foot sections at a rate of 30 yards per hour.

In that same year he made a patent application for improvements to agricultural steam engines and "locomotive engines for use on common roads", and three years later Smith and his partner John Birch Higgs made another application for improvements in "thrashing machines, and apparatus for raising or moving grain in granaries". Higgs was most likely related to Thomas Birch who was a lock-maker in the village in 1834 along with Smith senior and another man, James Roberts. There was a field named 'Higgs Meadow' very near to Lawn Farm at this time, perhaps it was in the Higgs family and was where Smith demonstrated his engine? John Smith senior also made patent applications for improvements

Figure 109: Frontispiece from The Gardens Of England

to threshing and grain drying machines in 1862/3.

Strong competition from Willenhall and Wolverhampton hastened the decline of the lock-making trade in Coven and Brewood from the middle of the century. For example, John Badger, a stock lock-maker at Coven Lawn, was declared bankrupt in 1854. He had lived on Coven Lawn since at least 1846 and at the 1851 census he was living with his wife and four children, brother Joseph, also a lock-maker, and three apprentices, most probably in one of the two cottages on the east side of Lawn Lane just south of Lawn Farm. The trade had been carried on in the area for at least 70 years beforehand however, as there is reference to James Aston, a locksmith of Brinsford in a deed of 1779. William Jackson was a lock-maker living at Dark Lane in the late 1830s - his was the isolated house opposite the present-day Sunnyside Dog's Home. The field behind his house was known as Rush Croft and at that time it was farmed by John Smith.

At the Staffordshire Agricultural Society's show in September 1856, Smith demonstrated his combined engine and threshing machine which created great interest and was said to go through its work with ease. He was awarded the top prize in the agricultural implements category of £2. Two years later the Society's show was held in the field above Lichfield railway station, and again John demonstrated his latest "excellent portable combined thrashing machine which could finish grain ready for market". He also entered one of his machines into the ploughing competition.

To give some idea of the price of this equipment, one of Smith's threshing machines, powered by a six horse-power engine with its own boiler, was advertised for sale at Rhyl in 1860; it had been purchased a little over a year beforehand at a price of £300, equivalent to tens of thousands of pounds today whichever means of calculation is used.

The Kentish Gazette of 20th December 1859 carried a large advertisement for the famous Aveling company, promoting themselves as agents for Fowler's Steam Ploughs. Fowler's mechanism consisted of two self-propelled engines, connected by cables, that moved slowly along opposite sides of a field. By means of a winch on each engine, a plough could be automatically drawn back and forth across the field, removing the need for horses.

The advertisement was a series of testimonial letters, one of which was sent by John Higgs; it praised the efficiency with which the plough could "smash up" a heavy clay field that no horse-drawn plough could cope with. Higgs also mentioned that he had connected one of the engines to a threshing machine. Another letter was addressed to 'John Smith, Engineer, Village Foundry, Coven', the sender again saying how satisfied he was with the engine he had purchased from Smith at the Warwickshire show. Smith was acting as an agent for the Aveling/Fowler ploughing equipment, powered by his own engines; he demonstrated this set up at a trial organised by Staffordshire Agricultural Society on the Bridgnorth Road in 1861.

In 1862 Smith was supposed to give a demonstration of Fowler's steam plough at the Staffordshire show, held at Newcastle Under Lyme. Unfortunately, the machine suffered accidental damage while being transported there by rail and was not operational on the opening day.

In the previous year, one of John Smith's traction engines was involved in a spectacular accident near the Bull Ring in Birmingham. The engine was being delivered to a customer in Stratford upon Avon and had in train half a dozen wagons loaded with agricultural implements. As it approached the Bull Ring at around 8 pm, there was confusion between the two men in charge of the locomotive about which way they should be going, and the lumbering giant ended up mounting the pavement and crashing through the front of Mr Gregory's boot shop! Had it travelled a few feet further it may have fallen through the flimsy floor into the cellar or demolished an iron pillar which supported the front of the building.

As the engine was travelling at low speed, the men aboard managed to jump clear before impact, but it took three hours, and the help of six Birmingham Corporation horses, before it was once more on its way. The accident is said to have attracted a huge crowd as such engines were still comparatively new and no doubt not often seen in the heart of the city. Whether Mr Smith had insurance to

FOWLER'S STEAM PLOUGH.

THE ABOVE ENGRAVING SHOWS THE POSITION OF THE STEAM PLOUGH WHEN WORKING.

Figure 110: Engraving that accompanied Aveling's advertisement in the Kentish Gazette.

cover an accident such as this is not known.

Smith's works, known as the 'Village Foundry', was built in 1857 and lay at the junction of Lawn Lane and the Brewood Road, in the place occupied today by 'Parson's Croft'. Somewhat confusingly, Mrs Ann Smith is listed amongst the 'gentry' in Harrison & Harrod's Directory & Gazetteer of Staffordshire (1861) as living at 'Coven House' but Coven House stood on the opposite side of Brewood Road to the Smith's foundry.

The foundry was probably built where it was because John Smith actually owned the land and it was adjacent to the family home. However, from a practical point of view it was inconveniently situated, having no direct rail or canal connection. This meant that incoming materials and outgoing engines had to move by road - a slow, difficult and expensive process - and this must have contributed to the downfall of the business.

In 1882, an enquiry into problems caused by traction engine traffic was held at Wolverhampton Town Hall. John Higgs, by then a traction engine proprietor, said that he used various sizes of engine to draw agricultural machinery from Coven to Wolverhampton station. Presumably he and Smith had done the same in the past as there was probably no way to load such heavy equipment at a

Figure 111: The Village Foundry in later years. A little of the Smith's cottage can be seen at the far right of the photograph.

Figure 112: Detail of the maker's plate from Smith's locomotive no. 122

Figure 113: John Smith's '122' locomotive, probably pictured at Willenhall (R. Shill)

small station like the much closer Four Ashes.

By the autumn of 1863 Smith and Higgs had built a number of locomotives for three Wolverhampton iron furnaces, one for Fletcher, Solly and Urwick's Willenhall works and two for the Chillington works. They were of varying specification but all had to cope with narrow-gauge track, gradients and tight curves, while pulling anything up to 100 tons of coal and ironstone. The typical speed of a fully laden train on such duties was in the region of 5-10 mph. The Willenhall works had at least three of Smith's engines, Rocket, Ajax and Vulcan. These last two were eventually converted to run on standard gauge track and went to the Hatherton Colliery, whereas Rocket may have gone to the River Weaver Trustees. In addition to these, Smith and Higgs supplied other railway engines to local collieries and ironworks further afield.

The partnership between Smith and Higgs was dissolved on 30th March 1864, ostensibly because of Smith's debts. A few weeks later Smith advertised for an engine-smith in the Birmingham Daily

Figure 114: 'Ajax' converted to standard gauge, pictured at Hatherton Colliery (Alex Appleton Collection)

Post, calling for "a thoroughly good workman, for locomotive and stationary engine work". Candidates were told to apply in person at the foundry.

John Smith senior was also interested in searching for coal deposits in Coven. In 1870 he wrote to the Institute of Mining, Civil and Mechanical Engineers saying that he owned land in the area and would be prepared to meet the cost of the first 100 yards of a trial shaft. His letter was passed to the president of the Institute who would have the final say in whether Smith's proposal would be accepted. Either it was rejected or the trial was unsuccessful as nothing more came of the matter.

In 1871 John Smith senior, still described as a farmer, was listed as head of the household at the Village Foundry, while his son was employing 22 men and boys in the engineering business. At least half a dozen men who were boiler-makers, engine-drivers or fitters lived just a few doors away from the works and were almost certainly among those employed by Smith. His works was capable of building a complete engine from scratch, including possibly the most difficult part, the boiler. By this time Higgs and family had moved to Kiddemore Green, Brewood.

John senior died on 8th September 1874. His wife, Mary Anne, son John and Wolverhampton ironworks manager John Wright proved the will.

In 1882, the fixtures and fittings of Willenhall Furnaces were put up for auction and two of Smith's coupled four-wheel tank engines were amongst the lots.

The output of John Smith junior has been examined in some detail in recent years by various researchers and a search of the Internet or local archives will provide more technical information about his various engines for those that are interested. John Smith senior was also involved in rivalry between the two public houses in the village, see the Public Houses chapter for more details.[34]

Michael Reynolds, The Engine Driver's Friend

Standeford was the birthplace of Michael Reynolds, a man who rose to become Locomotive Superintendent of the London Brighton and South Coast Railway and a prolific author. Probably his best known book, 'Engine Driving Life: Stirring Adventures and Incidents in the Lives of Locomotive Engine-Drivers', was completed at Standeford in November 1880.

Michael Reynolds' father and grandfather were both gardeners, but living a stone's throw from the railway and Four Ashes station when this means of transport was brand new, it is easy to imagine how the young man became absorbed by steam engines. From his home it would have been possible to get a long, uninterrupted view of trains passing along the embankment between Four Ashes and the canal bridge at Slade Heath. He would also have heard them chugging by at all times of day and night.

Before he became an engine driver, Reynolds was apprenticed to John Smith, the Coven locomotive builder and no doubt this gave him detailed insight into the construction and operation of

Figure 115: 'Grosvenor', the frontispiece from the original 'Engine Driving Life'.

steam locomotives. It was said that a journeyman who had served under John Smith would never have difficulty in securing another position if he desired a change. In one of his books written in later life, Reynolds harks back to these days when describing the position of the Locomotive Superintendent:

> In the locomotive department, the chief is the Locomotive Superintendent, who ranks as one of the highest officers in the railway service. His position requires that he should have received a thorough mechanical education, trained at the vice, and by experience. He is an engineer in every sense of the word, loving nothing better than engines, and able to hold his own on any locomotive question; and those under him with like talents receive their just reward.

Reynolds' exact address isn't given on the censuses, but in 1881 he was living with his aunt, Sarah Reynolds, and a lodger, physician William Hopkins. Whether or not Michael Reynolds ever married isn't clear; he is shown as married on this census, unmarried on that taken ten years later and married on the 1901 census, but there is no wife living with him on any of these!

In the original version of 'Stirring Adventures', which was reprinted in condensed form in the 1960s, Reynolds tells of his exploration of the railways near his home. He also relates the tragic tale of a local lad who was crushed when a gust of wind pinned him between the heavy shed door and an engine at Bushbury locomotive depot. Littleton Carless, the 15-year-old son of a railway 'plate-layer' of Slade Heath, was employed as a 'bar boy', a job reserved for young lads as they were required to climb inside the engine firebox to clean it.

After the accident Carless was taken to hospital, where an unsuccessful attempt was made to amputate his severely damaged arm, but he died as a result of his injuries and severe shock. An inquest was held the day before Christmas Eve 1870 and the unfortunate youth was buried at St Paul's three days later. Incidentally, it is quite possible that the Carless family were related to Colonel William Careless of Brewood, who famously assisted Charles II at Boscobel; the surname (in various forms) is often encountered when enquiring into the history of the area.

In 'Stirring Adventures', Reynolds uses many local place names as pseudonyms for various people and places, for example "driver Brewood" and "driver Somerford". In a chapter dealing with the Royal Train, driver Somerford is the engine-man in charge and he gives a long account of his engine and its preparedness. He mentions that a problem with the engine tender was resolved at Coven but this is most likely a substitution for some other place. No date is given for this episode and it seems improbable that the tender of such a prominent engine would have been repaired at Smith's Village Foundry (which had closed by 1874).

It does however seem reasonable, especially as the account is given in the first person, that driver Somerford was none other than Reynolds himself. In fact, at one point in his career, Michael Reynolds *was* driver of the famous 'Flying Scotsman' between London and Edinburgh. Being responsible for such a 'top link' express, it seems very likely that he would also have been a suitable candidate to take charge of Queen Victoria's train.

In 1894 it was revealed in the press that Reynolds had been working on a new type of engine that would break the landmark 100 mph barrier. With 10 foot driving wheels, a completely new type of boiler and twin chimneys, this radically different locomotive was said to be capable of great speed while offering a comfortable ride to passengers. The article claimed that the ladies of Stafford would find a one-hour-each-way shopping trip to London no more tiring than visiting Birmingham!

The locomotive was to be built by Dubs of Glasgow and the first trial run to be held on the Caledonian Railway but whether or not it ever took place is not known as there seems to be no trace of Reynold's engine amongst the company's lists. In any event the newspaper hedged its bets, saying that even if the trials were unsuccessful, they would no doubt contribute something to increasing the speed of locomotives.

Just after the turn of the century, Reynolds completed a paper detailing the life of William Stroudley, one of the most famous railway engineers of all time. Stroudley, who died about a decade beforehand, had worked for several of the major railway companies of the day, including the London & Brighton. An engraving of his prototype 'G' class express locomotive 'Grosvenor' forms the frontispiece of the original 'Engine Driving Life'.

It is safe to say that Michael Reynolds was a railway-man through and through; from his childhood spent near to the nascent Grand Junction, through his time with John Smith, his career as fireman, driver and senior engineer and in his prolific writing.

A browse through the 1911 census shows that there are a number of railway employees still in the Four Ashes and Standeford area, including plate-layers, station staff and engineers. No doubt many more Coven men and women worked at the large locomotive works at Stafford Road, the sheds at Bushbury and Oxley and the numerous nearby stations and yards.[35]

Dancing and Drama

Mr and Mrs Wynn of Somerford Hall were prominent members of the 'Coven Amateur Theatrical Party' and the 'Coven & District Social Club' during the 1920s.

As well as making the Hall available for rehearsals, they took roles in the group's performances and were involved in set creation, as were various members of the Banks family. The group performed at Penkridge and Bilbrook and one programme for their production of "Tilly Of Bloomsbury" shows that it was staged at the Victoria Hall in Darlaston.

The Wynns also hosted at least one evening 'Whist Drive', followed by dancing until midnight to the 'Ace of Clubs', a band made up of club members. This was held in the ballroom of Somerford Hall and the event must have had appeal beyond the immediate locality as buses were laid on at the end of the evening to take guests back to Wolverhampton. 'Conversaziones' were another regular social event in the life of this rather elite group of individuals.

Surnames

In his book 'In Search of England', historian and TV documentary maker, Michael Wood, tells how the surnames of some people in the Leicestershire village of Peatling Magna can be traced back as far as the early 1300s. While it's possible that a few Coven residents have surnames with equivalent longevity, even a casual inspection will show that certain distinctive names in this area crop up time and again over the last three or four hundred years.

A scan of the parish registers in the early 1600s shows some interesting surnames in Coven, although by then most had probably been in use for perhaps four generations. The following individuals were all inhabitants of Coven who were baptised, married or buried at Brewood (for there was no church at Coven), in the decades leading up to the English Civil War.

1608 Andrew Illedge - several generations with this surname

The Coven Club Amateur Theatrical Party
PRESENT

"ALADDIN"

A COMIC OPERETTA in three Acts.

ACT I.. SCENE I.—Widow Twankey's Kitchen.
    SCENE II.—The Cave.
    SCENE III.—Widow Twankey's Kitchen.
ACT II.   Court of the Emperor
ACT III., SCENE I.—Interior of Aladdin's Palace
    SCENE II.—The Plot of Ground where the vanished Palace had stood.
    SCENE III.—Interior of Aladdin's Palace.

Characters :

Aladdin	MISS F. WEBB
Widow Twankey (Aladdin's widowed Mother)	MR. A. R. WYNN
Abanazar (A wicked Magician)	MR. J. H. BANKS
The Emperor	MR. N. HUMPHREYS
The Princess, "Silver Moon" (The Emperor's daughter)	MISS G. E. BANKS
The Prime Minister, "Phatman"	MR. T. SHIPLEY
So So (His son)	MR. S. STEPHENS
Guards	MESSRS. EDWARDS and HILL
Genie of the Lamp	MISS C. BAILEY
Genie of the Ring	MISS C. BAILEY
Seraphina (Court Lady)	MISS D. DODD
Kanairi "	MISS M. JAROLD
Felicity "	MISS D. COLWICK
Sink-o-Fat (Courtier)	MR. H. DODD
Toedee "	MR. D. PARKER
Pinkoe "	MR. E. HUMPHREYS
Slaves of the Lamp	The MISSES L. TALBOTT, M. COURT, M. SMITH, M. WILLIAMS, L. ADAMS, E. CHETWOOD.

Stage Managers—MR. HUMPHREYS, SEN., & J. BAILEY, JUN.
Producer of the Play—MRS. G. STEPHENS.
Electrician—MR. H. HUMPHREYS
Pianist—MISS JESS. E. POWELL.
Dances arranged by—MISS F. HARRIS.
Scenery and Effects by—MRS. A. R. WYNN & MR. J. H. BANKS.

Programmes 2d. each.

G. H. Rowley & Son, Printers, Willenhall.

VICTORIA HALL
BOOTH STREET, DARLASTON

The Coven
Amateur Theatrical Party
present

Tilly of Bloomsbury
By IAN HAY

Thursday, October 31st, 1929.

PROGRAMME - 2d.

Figure 116: Programs for 'Tilly Of Bloomsbury' and 'Aladdin'.

appear in the parish registers and there is gravestone of Benjamin Ellidge of Coven who died in 1770. The 'Illedges' were farming at Grange Farm in Coven until at least 1800.

1610 John Cockett - a surname of uncertain origin.

1611 Richard Jeaven - (usually spelled Jeavon today) possibly of French origin and dating back to the conquest.

1612 John Brinsford - living at Brinsford, this locational surname might also be of considerable age.

1614 Richard Dutton - probably after the place in Cheshire.

1621 William Terry - ultimately believed to be derived from the ancient 'Theodoric'.

1623 Richard Tunckes - an unusual surname, there were also Tunckes at Shareshill around this time.

1625 William Weekes - another unusual name, may be derived from the Old English 'wic' meaning a hamlet or farm.

1625 William Blyth - of Scottish origin.

1625 John Arden - another locational name.

1627 Walter Cowly - or Cowley, again derived from a place name. Brewood Park Farm has a field named 'Cowley's Stile Leasow'.

1627 Henry Biddle - an uncommon name that can still be found in the area, having the same origins as the word 'beadle'.

1627 Agnes Floyd - said to be an English attempt to pronounce the Welsh 'Lloyd'.

1628 Jane Steene - another Scottish name.

1628 Thomas Pinke - an uncommon name, meaning happy, although it might be an association with the Penk.

1642 Thomas Spinke - derived from the Medieval name for a Chaffinch but this could be the same individual as above.

1642 Hugh Cowper - effectively the same as Cooper, i.e. a barrel maker.

Finally, a person with no surname, a foundling: baptised in 1617 'A certain child called Ann, whose father & mother we know not; the child was borne in the house of Thomas Floyde, of Coven.'

Possessions

While the ordinary folk of Coven in the seventeenth and eighteenth centuries probably had few personal possessions and creature comforts beyond the essentials, those at the wealthier end of the scale had sufficient furniture, soft furnishings and all manner of utensils to live a reasonably comfortable life.

An example of this can be seen in the inventory of Henry Richards' possessions, assembled and valued shortly after his death in 1672. Mr Richards was a 'yeoman farmer' who most likely lived at either Coven Farm or Grange Farm and who owned two or three properties, including a cottage "in or near Coven... called Paradice", and several fields.

> In the dwelling house, one Longe table, 6 Joyned Stooles, 3 Cheeres, one Iron Grate, with pottgeales [pot holders?], fyer Shovell and tongs
> In the parlour, one table, one livery Cubbard, one Joyned presse, with Stools and Cheeres amd other furniture
> In the Butterey, one table & 6 barrells
> In the best Chamber, one Joyned bedstid, one feather bed, two feaher boulsters, 2 pillowes, 2 blanketts, one coveringe, one payer of Curtaines & vallants, one livery Cubbard, one Round table, 2 Joyned Chests, 2 Cheeres, bed cord and matt
> In the inner Chamber, one halfe heads bedstids with a bed, 2 feather boulsters, 2 blanketts, one coveringe with Curtains and vallants, one table, one Coffer, 2 Cheeres, 3 Stooles and a warming pan.
> In the Chamber over the parlour, one Joyned bedstid, one halfe head bedstid, two feather beds, 4 feather boulsters, 4 blanketts, two Coverings, one payer of Curtains and vallants, one Joyned table, one Coffer, one Joyned box with bedcords and matts
> In the kitchen, all sorts of brasse & pewter with dreepinge pans, broaches, Racks and other necessarys used there
> In the house, all sorts of Linens and nappreware whatsoever

Corne and Maulte and all manner of provisions in the house
In the Barnes, all manner of Corne grain whatsoever, and Hay
Corne now groweinge on the grounds
4 Oxen
4 Cowes
4 twinters
2 yearlings
One yonge Nagge
One twinter Coulte
25 Sheepe
3 score swine
All sorts of poultry
Waynes, plowes, harrowes, yoakes, Chenes and all manner of Impleyments
Hempes, flax and all manner of Lumber, and all other goods not values or appraised before
His wareinge apparell and Readdy money in his purse

In 1802, the belongings of the late Mrs Powis, probably of The Croft, were sold at auction by Randle Walker of Wolverhampton. Items included in the sale show how farming was still inextricably linked to life at the heart of the village:

> "exceeding(ly) good feather beds, matrasses (sic), bedsteads with dimity and coloured cotton furniture, blankets, bedquilts, and counterpanes, several sets of elegant mahogany chairs, mahogany dining, pembroke, card, and pillar claw tables, mahogany double and single chests of drawers, pier and swing looking glass, eight day clock in oak case, large oak beaufet, sets of elegant china, flint and delph, floor and bedside carpets, silver tea and table spoons, great variety of kitchen requisites, copper furnace, pots, kettles, barrels, mashing tubs, and other useful brewing utensils.
> Very useful black mare rising six years old, fifteen hands, with light cart and gearing, chair, with cover and harness, cart, saddle and gearing, two barren cows, one

cow in calf, one new milch cow, one rearing cow calf, large quantity of manure, great variety of utensils for husbandry."[36]

Chapter 5
Making the News

Looking at the historic environment tells us plenty about the way our antecedents lived, but discovering the things that they did (or the things that were done to them!) can bring the past to life in a much more tangible form. While coal, carts and chickens are unlikely to make the news today, the family disputes, drunkenness and petty crime that also crop up in these stories could just as easily have happened last week as in the last century. So, it's time to look at some of the 'goings on' that would certainly have been discussed in the pub, at the butcher's shop, in a break from harvesting or in the smoky candle-lit parlours, of Coven in times past.

In most cases, names and other details have been quoted verbatim from newspaper reports, but where other more reliable sources exist, errors have been corrected.

Farming Woes

Trouble In Paradise

Edward Davies, a 41-year-old maltster, was employed by Mr Bickford at Paradise in 1884. In March he was moving a load of malt when his horse became restive and one of the cart shafts struck him in the side. He obviously suffered some serious internal injury, and complained of feeling pains in his side for two months after the accident, but he continued to work until the day he dropped down dead, on Sunday 18th May.[37]

In the summer of 1896 there was a serious outbreak of typhoid fever at Paradise; farmer William Bickford and his wife succumbed to the disease within a month of each other, leaving their son, also William, in charge of the farm.[38]

Brothers Joseph and Benjamin Morgan appeared in court in March 1908, charged with stealing a fowl from the Bickford's farm. In fact the bird had been killed by their dog but by keeping it, which they did not deny, they were found guilty of theft. Despite both men receiving good character references, the magistrate decided that they must pay costs but said that if they had not taken the dead fowl there would have been no charge to answer.[39]

On 1st October 1909, 15-year-old James Underwood from Bradley was spotted picking mushrooms in a field belonging to Henry Bickford at Paradise. When confronted, young Underwood became aggressive, broke some fencing, and bit Bickford's nephew, William Charles, on the hand! As Underwood did not appear at court a warrant was issued for his arrest but he does not seem to have been apprehended; there is no report of a trial and he does not appear in the area at the 1911 census.[40]

Cattle Plague

In the mid-1860s there was an outbreak of highly contagious 'Cattle Plague' or Rinderpest throughout Britain. This fatal disease permeated almost all parts of an infected animal and the airborne virus could be spread over a distance of 500 yards. In April 1866 Coven was declared infected and no cattle within a one mile radius of St Paul's church were allowed to move. It is only in the last few years that this terrible disease has finally been eradicated world-wide.[41]

Foot and Mouth

That other scourge of livestock, foot and mouth disease, necessitated similar restrictions on movement to minimise contagion. In

1870, William Bickford's farm at Paradise appeared in the newspaper lists of those afflicted. Twelve years later a zone stretching from Coven Heath to The Laches was designated as infected and, during another episode in the 1920s, John Frederick Owen, a farmer at Slade Heath, incurred a very heavy fine of over £100, for two counts of moving cattle without a license.[42]

Herbicidal Experiments

Brewood School had its own Agricultural Department in the nineteenth century and in the summer of 1889, students conducted experiments at various local farms in an effort to formulate a herbicide to eradicate 'Charlock' or 'wild mustard'. Once it gained a hold, this weed could completely choke the crop on any field and it was therefore a serious nuisance and threat to a farmer's livelihood.

Mr Keeling of Brewood Park Farm and Mr Bennett of Coven Heath provided afflicted J fields for the trials. The scientists discovered that a solution of copper sulphate, carried in a knapsack and sprayed through a machine known as a 'strawsometer', killed young plants and prevented flowering specimens from producing seeds. It was felt that annual treatment would be sufficient to completely eliminate the problem. The school must have been ahead of its time as chemical research into modern herbicides did not begin in earnest until the twentieth century and the same compound is still used as a weed-killer today.[43]

Checker And Timer, The Dangerous Poachers

A little after midnight on the first day of December 1876, three gamekeepers were watching land on the Monckton estate near Four Ashes. Head gamekeeper John Morrison and his colleagues Thomas Brew and George Cowley, were keeping an eye on two fields known as 'Old Lane Cover' and 'Harris' Leasow', when they spotted five men walking along the road, carrying bags over their shoulders. Strongly suspecting that the men were poachers, Morrison immediately sent Cowley to fetch his son from the keepers lodge on Deepmore Lane, and two other estate workers, all of whom soon arrived at the scene.

Morrison's suspicions were confirmed when the gamekeepers entered Harris' Leasow and they found the men setting out their nets. Morrison released his dog, which ran straight at the poachers, and he ran after it but became entangled in the nets. One of the poachers shouted out "Take your time, we are a match for you" and began throwing stones, several of which hit George Cowley and one knocked him down.

When Morrison finally managed to untangle himself, he and the two Cowleys approached the gang and, as they closed on them, one of the poachers shouted out "Loose it into 'em". Although it was very dark, as he was at almost point-blank range, Morrison could now see a gun pointed directly at his chest and moments later it was discharged. The shot missed Morrison's body but caught his left arm, causing serious injury.

Meanwhile, Cowley's son had been knocked down and was badly beaten by three of the poachers before they made their escape. Morrison was carried off to the Four Ashes Inn by Brew and the others and later that morning it became necessary to amputate his shattered arm above the elbow.

John Jones, a man of no fixed abode, was apprehended a little later in the day upon suspicion of being a member of the gang but the others seemed to have fled the area. Police enquiries identified one of the suspects: William Price, alias 'Checker', and he was arrested as he left Salford Gaol on Christmas Day. The Horsley Fields lodgings of one of his associates, Thomas Allman, alias 'Timer', had already been searched and traces of rabbit fur found in his clothing at the house. Allman himself was detained by police in Yorkshire and subsequently transferred to Stafford.

The men were committed for trial at the Stafford Quarter Sessions where Allman received 15 years penal servitude for the shooting, while Price and another man, Humphries, were each sentenced to five years for poaching. Two years later, another member of the gang, John Bennett alias 'Brummy', was apprehended near Manchester and he too was sent to Stafford for trial.

Poaching has of course gone on since time immemorial, often by local people in times of need, taking just the odd bird, rabbit or fish. One such case involved Thomas Jones of Coven Forge, who in 1797 was caught taking game at Chillington. He was summonsed to answer the charge at Stafford but whether he actually did so is not known. The mid-nineteenth century 'Chorus of Boatmen', which specifically mentions this area, does more than hint at illicitly obtained meat:[44]

> Gaily the fire in our caboose is crackling,
> Where many a rabbit and hare has been stewed,
> And many a hen has stopt short in her cackling,
> That wakened the echoes at Coven and Brewood.

Fire At Somerford

There was a fire at Somerford Farm, then in the tenancy of George Bickford, on a Saturday night in August 1911. The conflagration consumed six ricks of hay and corn and numerous pieces of farm equipment as well as badly damaging the Dutch barn in which they were stored. No cause for the fire could be identified but the losses, valued at around £550, were at least insured. It is interesting to note that the estate was able to deploy its own fire engine alongside that from the Brewood fire station.[45]

Grumbling Farmer

Charles Price, a Featherstone farmer, took one of his farm-hands to court at harvest-time in 1900. Herbert Hayward of Coven Heath was ordered to pay £2 10s 6d in total for 'neglecting his work' i.e. leaving without giving the required notice, in this case 14 days. Hayward complained that he had left because his boss was "always grumbling"![46]

The Village Bobby

The life of a village 'bobby' must have been pretty quiet at times, with nothing but the occasional theft, drunk or 'domestic' to deal with, as these typical events from the 1880s illustrate...

In 1883 P.C. McCabe found labourer John Bethell drunk inside a wicket gate on the road at Coven. He spent three hours trying to rouse the man before taking him back to his parent's home; a fine and costs totalling 11 shillings was imposed when the matter came to court.

Constable Spendlove was standing watching a hen making her nest at Beeches farm one day in March 1884. As he watched, Joseph George Wootton, a 15-year old lad who worked as a labourer on the farm, decided to help himself to three eggs from the hen house. It wasn't long before young Wootton found himself up before the magistrate where he was fined eightpence plus almost one pound in costs. At the Penkridge Petty Sessions, Brooke Chambley said he employed the youth at nine shillings a week and asked that Wootton be treated leniently as he had at least apologised for the theft. In the end, Wootton's older brother paid the fine and arranged for the lad to be sent back home to Herefordshire.

Farm labourers such as young Wootton were often hired at fairs and spent a year or more with the same farmer. Typically they would live in a barn or other farm building although they were well fed, usually taking meals in the farmhouse, often at the same table as the farmer and his family. Three decades before this event, four agricultural labourers were recorded as living in outbuildings at William Chambley's farm. Incidentally, William Chambley had himself brought cases for theft on at least two previous occasions - in 1838 against two men for stealing a shirt and in 1847 against a man for taking two quarts of milk.

In September 1884, labourer Thomas Grainger, was hauled before the Penkridge Petty Sessions for being drunk and riotous at Coven. Constable Price was witness to the event and Grainger was fined five shillings including costs.

On the 28th of the same month Charlotte Austins assaulted her mother-in-law, also named Charlotte Austins. The young Charlotte and her husband were living apart and she went to see if her husband was at his mother's house in the village. When she was told he wasn't there, she became abusive and pulled out some of the older woman's hair. Her temper cost her 14 days in prison with hard labour.

In December of the same year there was yet more excitement for the local constable, this time P.C. Hurmston, who saw celery being stolen from the garden of the Rainbow and duly made an arrest. At court in Cannock, publican Joseph Jackson was called to identify the celery as his property (!) and Thomas Leverton, alias 'Tater Tom', received 21 days imprisonment with hard labour. No information is forthcoming as to how Leverton got his nickname but it's fair to assume that the celery wasn't his first haul of vegetables!

In 1888 constables Lawson and Fletcher found John Pullen of Standeford Mill to be in a totally inebriated condition, just yards from his house at 10:30 pm. He had to be helped the short distance to his door by a friend but still managed to fall down three times before reaching it. Penkridge Police Court took a dim view and imposed a fine and costs of over ten shillings.[47]

Another local bobby, Constable Burton, made an important arrest in September 1895. He had been tipped off by colleagues in London that a man wanted for embezzlement since the previous December, had relatives in the Four Ashes area and may be inclined to call upon them at some point.

The fugitive, 31-year-old John Henry Reynolds, was a 'cutter out' in the clothing trade, who had absconded with over £200 from a tailor's club. It later transpired that Reynolds had persuaded a barmaid from Clapham to run away with him and set up business in Ilfracombe. His appearance was described as very gentlemanly, no doubt due to his tailoring knowledge and new found wealth! Fortunately, officer Burton had memorised a portrait of Reynolds published in the Police Gazette.

One evening Burton happened to attend the Parish Council meeting at Brewood, when he noticed that one of the auditors bore a striking resemblance to the wanted man. As the man left the meeting accompanied by friends, Burton approached and greeted him: "John Henry Reynolds?". Reynolds knew the game was up and admitted his identity straight away; a subsequent search of his lodgings turned up £155 of the missing money. He was taken back to London to stand trial at which he pleaded guilty.[48]

In the years either side of the First World War, another local Bobby, Constable Boyer, was most active along the Old Stafford Road between the Harrows and the Anchor. In October 1912 he reported one James Poultney, a Four Ashes labourer, for throwing a bottle into the road at about ten in the evening and refusing to pick it up; an act that led to a 10 shilling fine plus costs.

In the following month he collared two Penkridge labourers for being drunk and disorderly at Standeford at about eight in the evening. He was alerted to the incident by the shouting and swearing of a throng of people and when he arrived found four men involved in a fight, two of whom escaped. Each was again fined ten shillings.

In 1913 Boyer was enforcing a clamp-down on unlicensed dogs. John Willmer of Light Ash and Adeline Coleclough of Coven appeared at Penkridge Police Court on the same day and were each fined fifteen shillings plus costs. Mrs Coleclough told Boyer that she hadn't decided whether or not she was keeping the dog which was why she hadn't bought a license and she offered to pay on the spot. Her husband, who ran the brewery at the top of Lawn Lane, said that as the dog was a puppy, his wife didn't think she needed a license until it was nine months old anyway. Lord Hatherton told them they were defrauding ratepayers and had no valid excuse. The Colecloughs had five young children and no doubt they would have been quite certain about keeping the dog! Sadly, father and husband Frederick Coleclough died in April of the following year - the grave of Mr and Mrs Coleclough can be seen at St Paul's.

Frederick's brother and partner in the brewery, Henry Charles Coleclough, took his own life in 1899. At the inquest into his death, Frederick said that his brother was a very ambitious man, determined to make money at all costs. He said that Henry was convinced that everyone else was doing better than himself and he was constantly speculating but was never successful.

In the end it seems he had risked, and lost, his entire capital and in a state of depression shot himself. He was found on a footpath near Burton upon Trent, in possession of fifty cartridges and having shot himself through the mouth. The inquest jury returned a verdict of suicide while temporarily insane.

About 5:30 pm one day in May 1915, Constable Boyer was at Cross Green when he saw two men unloading coal from a boat belonging to H. S. Pitt & Co of Dudley. The men, Thomas Randle and Walter Sillwood, were depositing the coal in the outer yard of the Anchor Inn, from where the licensee, Frederick Hickman, was moving it into the inner yard.

When the officer questioned the men it became clear that they were stealing the coal and selling it on to Hickman. To make matters worse, Sillwood offered Boyer a drink if he would turn a blind eye to the offence, saying that he could "square it with the boss" (Hickman) and get a drink, even though it wasn't opening time. Randle pleaded with the constable saying that he would get the sack if the crime was reported. Hickman said he had learned his lesson and if Boyer wouldn't overlook the matter he would lose his license and his livelihood. The publican claimed he had only had "a bit" of coal off the men because his range was empty; it turned out that he had received around four hundredweight and paid four shillings for it!

In court it emerged that Randle and Sillwood had been transporting coal from Littleton Colliery back to their employer and had stopped at the Anchor when they saw Hickman in his stables and asked if he wanted any coal. Randle's employer said he had previously been of good character and would not be sacked - he was fined 40 shillings. Hickman, being in a responsible position was fined £7 but kept his license. Sillwood was not at court: he had enlisted in the meantime and was facing the music elsewhere.

In the middle of the War, Boyer was called to give evidence in a sheep-worrying case. A boy was walking a dog at Mount Pleasant when it broke free and attacked several sheep, causing the death of one adult and five lambs. The dog actually belonged to a Willenhall scrap dealer and it was therefore he who was summonsed to Penkridge Police Court and subsequently fined.

Eight years later Boyer was still working the same beat when he commandeered a motor car at Standeford to chase down a bicycle thief. The bike had been taken from Edwin Ward, who at one time was an assistant to the butcher, Stephen Kirk. The offender must have had considerable stamina, as it was not until they reached rising Brook, on the outskirts of Stafford, that the constable was able to apprehend him. The khaki-clad man was a Territorial soldier from Birmingham, named Harold Deakin. At court Lord Hatherton called for the man to be held in custody and to receive medical attention - perhaps he had served in the War and was still suffering as a result?[49]

Violence & Death

Housekeeper Drowned

In October 1831, the body of 52-year-old widow Sarah Mannington was found in the fourth pond of the Birmingham Canal. Mrs Mannington was housekeeper for Mr Leek, who lived near the 'Black Lion' at Slade Heath, and had been to Wolverhampton for supplies. Her body was discovered after her shopping basket was seen floating on the water.[50]

Evening Assault

Arthur and Joseph Sleith, both waggoners of Chillington Street, Coven, brought an assault charge against two Brewood men, Charles Brannon and Charles Muskin in September 1900. According to Joseph Sleith, he and his brother saw the defendants at about 8 o'clock in the evening of 19th August, and he wished them good night. He claimed that the pair abruptly turned around and one hit him on the side of the head and the other punched his brother in the chest.

The defendants denied the charge, claiming that Joseph Sleith had swore at them. One witness backed up the Sleith brothers while another testified for the defendants. In the absence of any other evidence the case was dismissed. Although listed under Coven in this instance, 'Chillington Street' is a track across Ackbury Heath on the far side of Port Lane.[51]

Infanticide At Coven Heath

On 12th April 1886 a baby girl was found in a drain at Coven Heath. The child had been strangled with a pocket handkerchief which was still tied around its neck. There is no report of the mother or the killer being identified.[52]

Domestic At Rock Bank

William Adams of Rock Bank was brought before the court in 1910 to face a charge of assaulting his wife. It seems the dispute arose over a lodger but, as no further detail is given in the newspaper reports, we will have to speculate upon the reason! He was bound over to keep the peace towards her for six months.[53]

Death Of A Hawker

Hawkers, traders who travelled from place to place selling their wares, were a familiar sight in previous centuries but 46-year-old Thomas Tomkinson of Stafford Street, Wolverhampton, was a little different to most. He was a cripple who got about by using a perambulator as a form of wheelchair. Sadly, his body was found in the canal at Coven Heath in August 1880 and, there being no evidence to the contrary, it was assumed that he had committed suicide.[54]

Father Loses His Temper

William Bryan, a railway plate-layer of Coven Heath, was found guilty of assaulting his daughter in August 1883. She had stayed away from home for two days against his wishes and when he took up the matter with her, he claimed she had used such bad language that it provoked the assault. The Wolverhampton court fined him £1 and he was bound over to keep the peace for a year.[55]

Canal Suicides

Emily Roberts, from a well respected Slade Heath family, had been travelling in Europe as a ladies companion. By February 1908 she had returned to England, after suffering a nervous breakdown, and was an inmate at a nursing institution in Wolverhampton. Despite her fragile condition, she was due to be married on the 20th February but the event never came to pass. On the 19th her body was found in the canal at Slade Heath - she had left a note saying that her body would be found near her home.

Emily Bailey drowned herself and her 6-year-old daughter Violet, in the canal at Four Ashes in 1907. She first threw Violet into the water then tried to throw in her elder daughter, Alice, but the girl ran off screaming and raised the alarm with her father. By the time he got to the spot, mother and daughter were dead. The coroner's inquest held at the Four Ashes returned a verdict of "suicide and wilful murder while temporarily insane".[56]

Skeleton In The Woods

In late 1922, the decomposed body of a young woman was found in woodland near Four Ashes by a gamekeeper. A neatly folded pile of clothes, a hat and pair of boots lay a few yards from the body, which was little more than a skeleton. Fortunately, identification was simple because name tags had been sewn into the woman's clothing. Close to the body lay an empty quart wine bottle and some unspent matches, but whether these were in some way related to the death could not be determined. To quote one account "it was as if the young woman had lain down in her underwear and gone to sleep".

The girl was nineteen-year-old Pauline Mildred Cadwallader, a domestic servant for a Mrs Burt at Oxley. She had been missing for a couple of months, having last been seen by a policeman at Four Ashes station in mid-August, apparently intending to take a train to Wolverhampton. Her father, a gardener on the Somerford estate, said that she was a bright and cheerful girl and, as far as he knew, had no male friends. He said she was familiar with the wood but was much too timid to enter it alone.

When interviewed, Mrs Burt said that a well-dressed young man had called to see Miss Cadwallader over a year beforehand, but said they had not gone out together. She also said that she had received a letter from Pauline on the day after she left her service. It was postmarked Stretton and contained nothing but money.

It seemed that Miss Cadwallader may have taken her own life, as according to Mrs Burt, the girl was fascinated by accounts of murder and suicide. On one occasion, when discussing a local suicide, she even suggested the concoction that may have been used. Mrs Burt's daughter said that Pauline would often go off into the woods on her own to read about such cases. A night-watchman told the coroner's inquest that Cadwallader had called at his box on the Stafford Road one night in the middle of August, around midnight. She warmed herself by the fire and accepted a cup of tea, telling him that she was writing a story about her life. The inquest returned a verdict of "found dead" - too little of the body remained to determine the exact cause of death.

Miss Cadwallader's corpse was taken to the Four Ashes Inn when it was discovered. Annie Elizabeth Kirk ran the pub at that time and her daughter, who was in her mid-twenties, recalled the details of this grisly event some years later:

> I slept in the four poster bed for years, my bedroom was over the stable, it was so cold and the horses used to kick all night. When it was wet the policemen used

to go in there and stand and talk. Once we had a dead girl in there for a week - it was a skeleton, you could smell it up in the bedroom, it had that earthy smell. When a dead body was found in those days it had to go straight to the nearest Public House. It happened in the November, on a Wednesday, when they had all gone to town and mother and I were alone. A policeman came up and wanted a door to put this body on and they put her in the stable. She was wearing a slave bangle and that was how they identified the body. She had taken some poison and her name was Pauline Cadwallader and she was a maid at Bushbury. She had been keeping the milk money - she had been home for the weekend and was afraid to go back. That was in the August and the keeper found her under a bush in the big wood at Somerford in the November. She was a girl of about twenty. The inquest was held in our tea room, the one over the kitchen.

This fascinating account seems to offer a reason for the teenager having taken her own life and to explain the money received by Mrs Burt - details which were not reported in the newspapers at the time.[57]

The Waggoner And The Draper

One early June evening in 1884, Charles Walter Clarkson, a 26-year-old draper and tailor with premises at Blakenhall and Brewood, visited Richard Oakley at The Laches . In the course of their meeting, Oakley asked Clarkson if he had seen one of his employees, Thomas Gallimore, a man in his forties, who worked for him as a waggoner. Clarkson said that he had seen him earlier in the day at Oxley, that he was the worse for drink and that it would "take some soda to put him right".

By all accounts this wasn't out of the ordinary for Gallimore, although Oakley later said that he was a good worker with the strength of two men when sober. Oakley sent Mrs Gallimore to bring back her husband and when they returned, Oakley told Gallimore that Clarkson has seen him at Oxley. Thinking that Clarkson had been talking about him behind his back, Gallimore threatened to "spoil the looks of him to go back to Wolverhampton".

The next day Gallimore bumped into Clarkson at Brewood and demanded to know what he had been saying about him to his employer. An argument ensued and a fight soon broke out which ended when Clarkson struck the older man with the handle of his riding whip. The handle, being of solid bone, made an inch long cut on the side of Gallimore's face.

Mrs Gallimore saw her husband at Oakley's stables that evening and the wound was still bleeding profusely. Clarkson was also at Oakley's house and Mrs Gallimore confronted him saying "Do you reckon yourself a gentleman?", to which he replied "No, I am very sorry for what I have done. Take him to the doctors and I will pay all the expenses".

Clarkson told Mrs Gallimore to hire a trap to take her husband to Mr Duce, the local doctor, but she was still enraged and called out "You have killed my husband and will have to keep me as a widow". Although her husband was alive, she believed that he was bleeding so badly that he would bleed to death. As Clarkson left, the frantic woman pelted him with stones.

By the time she got her husband to the Doctor, Clarkson was already there waiting and had told Mr Duce exactly what had happened. Mr Duce treated the injury and the matter was supposedly closed, but a couple of days later Gallimore obtained a certificate from Mr Duce in order to press a charge of assault at Penkridge Police Court. In the event this charge was dismissed as Clarkson was adjudged to have acted in self defence. Later that same day however, Gallimore's conditioned worsened and lockjaw set in. Despite Duce's best efforts, Gallimore died four days later.

Duce, and Brewood surgeon Mr Worthing, carried out a post mortem and found that the wound itself was very slight with no associated fracture. In their opinion, Gallimore's trip from his home at Slade Heath to Penkridge Police Court had not made any difference to his condition, he died purely as a result of tetanus infection.

An inquest was held at 'The Harrow', and the jury, having gone into the events in minute detail, decided upon a verdict of justifiable homicide. Clarkson, it seems, was truly sorry for his actions and had made reparation to Mrs Gallimore even before the inquest.

Gallimore seems to have been a man after his master's heart - four years after this event Richard Oakley was himself charged with drunkenness after visiting the Rainbow.[58]

Demon Drink

Locked Up

George Carter left the Anchor Inn 'the worse for wear' on 15th January 1900 and tried to drive away his cart-load of coal. Constable Poulton however, decided that the man was in no fit state to do so and, after locking him up, took the vehicle to the man's house at Coven Heath. Carter was fined just under six shillings at Penkridge Police Court a few days later.[59]

Attempted Suicide?

Police Sergeant Bond found Kate Taylor standing beside the canal at Coven on 27th October 1894. She was in a drunken state, with a bottle of whiskey concealed under her shawl, and her clothes were soaking wet. Sergeant Bond took her into custody and she duly appeared at Penkridge Police Court charged with attempted suicide.

She told the magistrate that she had worked as a housekeeper but since her master had taken a new wife she was no longer required. She said she had no friends that could help her but nevertheless denied trying to take her own life; she claimed that she had accidentally fallen into the water and struggled out again. She was fined a shilling plus costs or seven days in prison. Realising her predicament however, the magistrate said he would see what could be done to help her in the meantime.[60]

Determined Drunk

In June 1895 the landlord at the Four Ashes refused to serve Hardwick Simpson because he had already had more than enough to drink. Constable Barnett overheard the exchange and told Simpson, who worked as a clerk at Wolverhampton, to go home. After hanging around for a while he finally seemed to have taken the officer's advice and disappeared.

A little later, as Barnett was passing the Harrow Inn, he saw Simpson outside surrounded by a group of people. Simpson was cursing and said he was going to "drink four gallons". When he refused to leave the vicinity and go home Barnett had no choice but to lock him up for the night. At Penkridge Petty Sessions, a fine and costs totalling 8 shillings and sixpence were imposed.[61]

Skin-Full & Foul Mouth

Just over a week into the twentieth century, two locals found themselves at Penkridge Police Court - Joseph Plant for being drunk and disorderly at Coven a day or two before Christmas, and George Faulkner of Coven Heath for using obscene language. Constable Poulton provided the evidence in both cases and each man was fined over a shilling.[62]

Lost His Hat

Alfred Ward was summonsed for being drunk and disorderly outside the Rainbow on Boxing Day 1913. When P.C. Snead was called to the scene (just a few yards from the Police Station, housed in 'The Homage'), he found the landlord on his doorstep, refusing to let Ward in. Ward claimed that two of his friends, who were inside the pub, had his hat and he wanted it back. Constable Snead looked inside the pub but despite no-one being found, Ward refused to leave the scene for some time. On this occasion, Ward escaped without conviction although he was ordered to pay costs.[63]

Transport Trouble

Rock Bank Bicycle Con

James Jones, a labourer who lived at 'Rat Bank' (Rock Bank, Mount Pleasant) in 1902, managed to obtain money by deception from two local men within a few days of each other.

Firstly he approached Ashton Veall, an architect who lived at Brewood, and asked for help with a fine he had to pay for riding his bike at Penkridge without a light. Veall lent him two shillings and sixpence on condition that it was repaid within a week. Just three days later however, Jones used a similar ploy to obtain a further two shillings from Henry Nicholls who lived at Lower Green, promising once again to repay promptly.

Nicholls was in his mid fifties and sufficiently wealthy to be living on his own means. Although he was trusting enough to lend Jones the money, he must have smelled a rat, as he somehow uncovered the ruse and went straight to the police. After appearing at Penkridge Police Court Jones found himself with a real fine and costs totalling thirty two shillings![64]

Nameless Wagon

In 1890, Richard Waring, a Standeford farmer, was summonsed for allowing the owner's nameplate on his wagon to become illegible. A fine of 5 shillings and the cost of the case was imposed.[65]

No Documents

James Dudfield, a Gloucester hay dealer, was fined ten shillings plus costs in 1904. The case was brought because he failed to produce the necessary documents for his canal boat while it was moored at Coven. Registration and regular inspection for any boat that had accommodation, had been a requirement since an Act of 1877.[66]

Crash At Coven

Just before the outbreak of World War One, Arthur Beddard, a young engineer of Slade Heath, took James Gamson to court to claim damages as a result of 'negligent driving'. Beddard had been out on his motorbike, with a friend riding pillion, accompanied by another motorcyclist. Before taking a bend in the road at Coven, the motorcyclists sounded their horns, as was required by law, but as they rounded the corner they came face-to-face with Gamson's cart which was on the wrong side of the road. In the ensuing collision, Beddard was thrown from his bike and knocked unconscious, a condition in which he remained for the following three days.

Immediately after the crash, Gamson got down from his cart, tore off his jacket and threw it into a hedge, then challenged anyone present to a fight! When a young woman who was passing told him there was "a man dying in the road", Gamson refused to help, saying "let him die, I ought to have killed him".

When the village constable arrived at the scene he found that Gamson, a carrier of Newport Street, Brewood, was drunk. Nevertheless, when the case came to court, Gamson claimed that he was on the right side of the road and that the motorcyclists had been racing each other. Judge and jury did not agree and Beddard was awarded £7 10s; rather less than the £25 he was claiming for an injured knee and concussion.

James Gamson ran a single afternoon service as a market carrier from the The Fox in North Street, Wolverhampton, to Brewood on Mondays, Wednesdays and Saturdays. In addition to being a carrier and coal dealer, he and his wife also ran a bakers shop at Newport Street. A postcard featuring the family in front of this shop is held at the William Salt Library.

Gamson was said to be a man who liked to play tricks on people. While on the road he would frequently tell people that he had just come from the 'Four Ashes' and that Mr Kirk wanted to see them. The hapless victim would hurry along to the pub only to be greeted by a nonplussed publican!

Dorothy Dodd noted in her recollections of growing up in Coven at this time, that when they went to town at Christmas, they would get there in a carrier's cart, sitting amongst the vegetables and dead rabbits. On the return journey they would rely on the horse to find its own way home, the driver often being incapable through drink.

It was also said that if a woman borrowed her husband's pony and trap she could tell which pubs he frequented, as the horse would pull-in to each of its own accord![67]

Run Over

Thirteen-year-old Alfred Davis of Coven Heath was run over and killed while in charge of a horse and cart at Bushbury in 1890. A verdict of accidental death was returned by the inquest jury. [68]

Bikes on The Pavement

In the summer of 1889 five men from a group of about twenty were brought up at the Penkridge Petty Sessions to answer a charge of riding on the footpath between Standeford and Coven. There was no argument about the facts but the cyclists, from Wednesbury and Wolverhampton, claimed they were on the path because the road was in such a poor state of repair. The case was dismissed but they were each required to pay costs of eight shillings.

Five years earlier, eighteen-year-old Robert Keeling of Brewood Park Farm was fined a shilling for riding on the pavement at Brewood.[69]

Oddities

Baker's Bun In The Oven

Coven baker Alfred Ward (probably he of the lost hat, mentioned above, although there were two men of this name in Coven) was brought to court by Florence Hood in 1911 because he refused to pay maintenance for their illegitimate child. After hearing evidence the bench decided that he must pay two shillings and sixpence a week until the child reached the age of fourteen. As noted earlier, he still seems to have had sufficient money to enjoy Christmas 1913![70]

Love Labourer Lost

Frederick Broadbent, a labourer who lived at Cinder Hill, was similarly summonsed by Sarah Elizabeth Ward of Standeford. Only two years had elapsed since the previous case involving Alfred Ward but the levy was now three shillings for fourteen years.[71]

En-rag-ed By A Dog

In 1909 a 20-year-old rag-man named William Griffiths had his trousers torn by the schoolmaster's dog, while plying his trade in Coven. As he passed the schoolhouse for a second time a little later in the day, one of the schoolmaster's servants laughed at him. Griffiths became enraged and threw a rock at the dog which caused such serious injury to its skull that it had to be destroyed. Following a court appearance, Griffiths was ordered to pay some 17 shillings in fines and costs.[72]

Rent Overdue

In 1876 Francis Monckton took William Perks to court to recover six years worth of rent in respect of land and buildings at Lower Green. The demise had been settled on Perks, an iron-founder of Waterloo Road, Wolverhampton, in the will of James Roberts. Monckton had brought the matter to court a year earlier but could not prove that Roberts was actually the tenant so the case had been dismissed. In the intervening period, Monckton managed to contact his former rent collector, a Mr Mein, who was able to produce a rent book showing that Roberts had indeed paid rent, albeit back in 1863, proving once and for all that he, and therefore Perks, was the tenant.

At the judge's suggestion, the lawyers for each party consulted one another and shortly declared that an amicable solution had been found; Perks would remain as tenant for the rest of his life at a nominal rent and each party would meet their own costs.[73]

Busy Lady

In 1804 a short newspaper article entitled 'Instance of Industry' described part of the daily routine of one Phoebe Bate, wife of a Coven shoemaker. She walked a round-trip of four miles twice a day to milk two cows and it was calculated that she had therefore walked over 1400 miles, and spent the equivalent of 4 weeks doing so, in just six months.

Despite this call on her time, it was said that Mrs Bate, her house and *eleven* children were in no way neglected![74]

Standeford Stamina

Michael Lovatt, a Standeford farmer, died after "a few hours indisposition" in May 1830. Mr Lovatt was described as an honest and industrious man, a good father, husband and neighbour, who was universally respected. On the day before died, he walked to Wolverhampton and back then went off to work in his fields as usual - he was 79 years old. His son Richard continued to farm there and in 1851 he and Michael Reynolds' family were neighbours.[75]

Earthquake

In 1678, the year before the Homage was built, there was a strong earthquake which seems to have had its epicentre in the vicinity of Coven. On the night of November 4th there was a succession of quakes, accompanied by thunderous noise, every half an hour from 11 pm until 2 am the next morning.

Less intense aftershocks were felt on the following evening, adding an unusual accompaniment to Guy Fawkes Night![76]

Rich Tramp

In the summer of 1883, John Comings appeared at Wolverhampton Police Court charged with sleeping in a barn at Coven Heath. The police officer who discovered the tramp found that he was carrying no less than 49 half crowns and other money totalling over £6. Comings was let off with a small fine which, needless to say, he was able to pay immediately! [77]

Expensive Chestnuts

Seventeen year old Charles 'Charley' Pacey, who lived with his family as Aspley Cottages in 1909, was fined over ten shillings for throwing stones at a chestnut tree at Standeford! Some of the stones had fallen in the road and others in someone's garden.[78]

A Nuisance To The Neighbourhood

A little after eleven in the evening on Boxing Day 1912, Albert Richard Genner of Lower Green was arrested for causing a disturbance and using obscene language in the village. Genner, who was in his mid-forties, was late arriving at his court hearing, held at Penkridge in January, and so did not hear Constable Boyer describing him as "a nuisance to the neighbourhood".

Lord Hatherton asked if Genner was sober, to which Boyer replied in the affirmative. Asked if Genner was sane, Boyer declared that he could not say. Constable Snead generated considerable laughter in the courtroom when asked the same question, by responding "No sir, he is married"!

Boyer said that the fracas was the result of a family disagreement and this was corroborated by a neighbour, Fred Peake. Mr Peake said that in the past, he and his brother had been threatened by Genner, who owned a muzzle loading gun and had told Peake he "knew a trick how to poison everyone in Coven".

When Genner finally arrived at court, the case was explained to him but he denied using any threats. He was fined a shilling for his disorderly conduct and fined £5 and bound over for six months for threatening behaviour.

A year beforehand, Genner's wife Sarah Ann, had been fined for stealing three mangolds (a leafy vegetable, also known as chard) from Henry Bickford of Paradise Farm. She admitted the offence, saying that she did not have enough money to buy food for her pigs.

In 1915 she was fined 30 shillings for keeping a carriage without a license, constables Boyer and Snead once more providing the evidence.

Seven years later, Mrs Genner, now widowed, was brought before the police court yet again, this time on a charge of causing unnecessary suffering to nine pigs. The animals were found to be seriously undernourished by RSPCA inspectors although Mrs Genner claimed that they "had a cold" and she was treating them for it. Lord Hatherton was singularly unimpressed, especially as she had a previous conviction for the same offence. He imposed a £5 fine. [79]

Attempted Poisoning

Ruth Cartmail was born in Coven in 1890 and lived with her family near the Four Ashes Inn, until she entered service for a family at Solihull in 1906. Early one morning, when she was called to light the fire by her master, there was no answer. A message was found, on a table downstairs, which read: "You'll find me in the cellar dead. I've put poison in the porridge".

The cellar door was locked, but when broken open there was no trace of the young woman. The porridge however, had been clumsily poisoned by soaking a box of phosphorous matches in it. The matter was passed to the police and Miss Cartmail was soon apprehended on the Stratford Road, having been wandering the lanes around Solihull and Shirley in the meantime. She was remanded in order that her mental state could be assessed.

The outcome of the episode is not known, but a couple of years later she married local woodsman George Powell and the couple settled down at Standeford.[80]

Prize Punch-Up

In 1868, two bare-knuckle prize-fighters, Peter Morris and Henry Taylor, both of Birmingham, arranged for a fight to be held at Four Ashes. The pugilists, accompanied by a group of men, set off from Birmingham by train but the police had somehow got wind of the fight and swooped as the ring was being set up. They managed to seize a large part of the money that had been bet and Morris was taken into custody. Taylor, however, managed to escape by the simple expedient of a change of clothes! Morris was bound over for twelve months with sureties of £40.

These illicit fights seem to have been going on in this area for several years beforehand, probably because the railway offered contestants and punters a means to get out of the nearby towns and away from the eyes of the law. Despite being illegal, matches were still reported in detail in the newspapers, often accompanied by a description of how well the police had done in breaking up the meetings and making arrests![81]

Cases of Theft & Fraud

Ate His Fill

In 1827 a stout young man called at the Four Ashes and ordered six bread rolls, a pound of cheese and a quart of ale. After downing his beer and eating half the food he made to leave without paying. When landlord Joseph Ward remonstrated with him, he replied that he had no money and would never have got such a good meal by begging! Although the story sounds apocryphal, it was reported far afield and the details were quite specific.[82]

Stolen Ducks

In the winter of 1879, John Gamble and Richard Spruce were each sentenced to six months imprisonment with hard labour, for stealing three ducks belonging to Joseph and Charlotte Hinks (or Hincks) who lived in Coven House, opposite the top of Lawn Lane. On the night of 5th January, Mrs Hinks was woken by noises in the garden. She opened the bedroom window and saw two men in the garden, one of whom had some ducks under his arm. When she called out the men ran away and in the morning the ducks were found to be missing. The police were informed, the men soon arrested and the ducks recovered.

Richard Spruce and his family lived near the canal at Slade Heath in 1871, at which time he was supporting his wife, five children (three from his wife's previous marriage) and his younger brother. Spruce was a boiler maker by trade, perhaps he worked for John Smith at the village foundry (which closed in the mid 70s) and had fallen upon hard times? Pure speculation, but the sentence must have inflicted considerable hardship upon his family in any event. [83]

The Cheating Curate

Reverend George Elliott called on Coven Heath farmer George Vaughan to ask if he would contribute towards a fund for soldiers disabled as a result of the recent war in Egypt. Elliott told Mr Vaughan that he was acting curate for the vicar of Bushbury, and on the strength of this, Mr Vaughan gave him a shilling. When the farmer later discovered that Elliott was unknown to the minister at Bushbury, he called in the police.

When apprehended by Sergeant Woodhouse, Elliott was completely inebriated and it transpired that he had made the same representations to Mrs Smith of Oxley Lodge and to a Mrs Causer of Bushbury, as he had to Vaughan. The matter came to court in January 1883 with Elliott facing a charge of obtaining money by false pretences.

In his defence Elliott said that he had told Vaughan that he was acting curate for a *former* vicar of Bushbury, not the present one. He was able to produce a number of character witnesses and proof from the War Office that he was authorised to collect funds, although he had not yet returned any of the money he had collected!

He also produced evidence that he had contracted Yellow Fever whilst in the West Indies and, as a result, was sometimes not responsible for his actions. Despite this and his offer to pay back the money, the magistrates must have had their suspicions and convicted him under the Vagrancy Act, imposing a fine of £5 or a month in prison in default. [84]

Teenager Transported

In 1830, 14-year-old Elizabeth Brough was charged with stealing fifteen shillings from Ann Russell and a quantity of clothing from John Adie at Coven. She was acquitted of the latter but transported for seven years for the former. [85]

The Damson Wine Thieves

Arthur Price and James Flemming were each fined sixteen shillings for stealing damson wine belonging to Mary Hemmingsley of Slade Heath in October 1889. The men, who both lived at Monument Road, Birmingham, were bridge painters. They were lodging at Mrs Hemmingsley's house and may have been working on the cast iron bridge, which at that time carried the railway over the canal.

She also accused them of stealing half a dozen items of gold jewellery, a pocket knife and a marriage certificate(!).

When the men were apprehended by Constable Maguire of Coven, they admitted taking the wine but denied stealing the other items and maintained this stance when the matter came to court. No evidence could be produced to show that they had taken anything except the wine, hence the comparatively light fine. [86]

Attempted Robbery

In 1828 William Charles Willetts, aged 43, was found guilty of attempted robbery from Thomas James at Coven and received a sentence of two months prison with hard labour. [87]

Corn Thief

Charles Bird of Slade Heath managed the distribution of corn at the Coppice Colliery, Cheslyn Hay, in the years just after the Great War. He used his position to coerce two boatmen, John Harris and William Robinson, into transporting stolen sacks of corn on his behalf and delivering them to his home at Slade Heath.

The usual ploy was for Bird to hide a sack of corn amongst his legitimate coal allowance, ready for delivery to his home by canal. The boatmen would pull up outside his canal-side house and give a whistle, whereupon Mrs Bird and her sister would appear, load the corn into a wheelbarrow and take it into the house.

On 17th January 1921 however, whether by luck or prior knowledge, Constable Boyer was in place to see the furtive unloading. All those involved were subsequently brought before the Police Court at Penkridge, to answer charges of theft and receiving stolen goods. Bird was fined £20 for each of three thefts, his wife Zilpah and the others receiving smaller but not insubstantial fines for their involvement.[88]

The Butcher's Horse & Trap

Charles Henry Steer, a travelling mineral-water salesman from Wolverhampton seemed to prefer a stronger drink for himself. In March 1893 he took a horse and trap from outside the George & Fox at Penkridge and set off in the direction of Cannock. Not only was he completely befuddled with drink but he was seen repeatedly striking the horse with the stock of a whip.

The horse and trap belonged to John Yeomans, who ran the butchers shop beside the family farm at Mount Pleasant, Coven.

Steer was caught in possession of the vehicle later in the day, while heading back towards Penkridge, and finally ended up with a thirty shilling fine for drunkenness and cruelty - a charge of theft was dismissed.[89]

Head Office Hovel

The honourable sounding 'Wolverhampton and Birmingham Loyal Carters Sick and Burial Benefit Society' supposedly had its offices at Bilston Street, Wolverhampton. When detectives discovered that the society didn't actually exist and that one of its principal Directors, Dr Crockett of Darlington Street, had never even heard of it, they began a fraud enquiry.

It didn't take long for them to arrest the perpetrator, who seems to have been turned-in by his wife. Edward Jones was a fifty-year-old farm labourer and the bogus insurance company's 'Head Office' was in fact a hut in a potato field at Coven! In this "hovel" the police found a number of fake ledgers and over eighty insurance collecting cards. Jones must have been able to present a believable appearance to accompany his sham credentials, as he defrauded a considerable number of individuals. When arrested he confessed straight away, saying "Yes, I'm the man. The society is in a flourishing condition. I am open to all-comers. You would not have known anything about this if it had not been for my wife. I have got her to thank for this".[90]

Chapter 6
Public Houses

All of the present-day public houses in and around Coven were in existence by the 1830s, but there were three others; the New Inn within the village and the Black Lion at Slade Heath, both of which disappeared more than a hundred years ago, and the Golden Ball, at Coven Heath, which was demolished around 1981. In addition to these pubs, during the middle part of the nineteenth century there were several 'beer-houses', ordinary residential dwellings from which beer was sold.

In the past, public houses were used for many purposes other than the consumption of alcohol. In particular, they were frequently used for coroner's inquests, meetings, and auctions as there was often no other suitable venue in a locality. Although towns might have halls, church buildings and schools that could be pressed into service to meet these needs, public houses were often preferred simply for convenience. Away from the towns, in villages such as Coven, there was little alternative. It was also common for publicans to have another occupation, such as a farmer or blacksmith, so that one trade would supplement the other.

Public houses played a pivotal role in the life of the locality, not only in providing one of the few legitimate forms of entertainment, but as a focus for events good and bad; there is barely a story about Coven in the 1800s that doesn't mention one of them at some point! As well as serving the inhabitants of the village and nearby hamlets, they also met the needs of those using the various thoroughfares that lay close by, be it the Stafford Road, the Grand Junction railway or the Staffordshire and Worcestershire canal.

The fortunes of our local public houses waxed and waned in the past just as they do today and they rarely remained in the same hands for more than a decade at a time, sometimes changing tenancy every few years. Then as now, they served as meeting points for clubs and societies, and as venues for sporting events, functions, auctions and even inquests. Though they make strange bed-fellows, pub and church can lay equal claim to having been at the heart of local life for the last two hundred years.

The Black Lion

The Black Lion Inn was a public house on the Old Stafford Road at Slade Heath. As noted above, in the nineteenth century it was not uncommon for inn-keepers to have other occupations and in 1834, the keeper of the Black Lion, James Haden, was also a rope-maker. His premises beside the Staffordshire and Worcestershire Canal must have been the ideal place to carry on these two trades!

A long thin strip of land adjacent to the Stafford Road, between the canal bridge and The Black Lion, was the 'ropewalk', an area where individual strands of rope could be laid out, ready to be twisted into the finished product. This site may have included some form of shelter but was more likely just a flat or paved area on which the required trestles and winding equipment could be set out. Tow lines and other ropes were in constant demand by boatmen as the combination of water, dirt and the forces involved in pulling (and slowing) boats caused them to wear out very quickly. The wharf, which provided access to the inn and the rope works, is still in use today for leisure craft.

The field on the opposite, south, side of the Black Lion was known as 'Leek's Slade Heath Piece'. Edward Leek, who lived opposite the field, was Mr Haden's nearest neighbour, but whether or not this field and 'Leeks House Close' near Jackson's Bridge were anything to do with him is uncertain.

In the four years from 1837, the inn was peripherally involved in no less than three court cases, although by this time James Glover, born around 1787 at Brewood, was the inn-keeper.

In June 1837 Glover was the victim of a 'highway robbery'. He had received payment of more than £3 at Wolverhampton for work done on the Grand Junction Railway and decided to stop off at 'The Fox', on Stafford Street, on his way home.

After having a few drinks, Glover carelessly revealed his money and said that he was afraid to go home at such a late hour for fear of being robbed. Little did he know that several bad characters, including Abraham Powers, a member of the locally notorious 'thimble-rig gang', had overheard his indiscretion.

Glover left the pub some time after midnight but before he had travelled very far he was accosted by three or four men and beaten to the ground. His money was taken, along with some tea and coffee he was carrying. At the initial hearing Powers was discharged as, perhaps unsurprisingly, no one could be found to identify him. Four other men were committed and stood trial at Stafford later that month.

At the trial, a young apprentice named Pawton gave evidence against the prisoners. He had suspected they were up to no good and had watched them from a distance. He caused laughter in the courtroom when, referring to Glover's condition, he said that they did not consider a man drunk in Wolverhampton until he needed someone to lead him home. As positive identification was not forthcoming for all of the accused, only two, Jones and Selvey, were found guilty and sentenced to twelve months hard labour.

As the Grand Junction was still under construction in 1837 it may be that Mr Glover supplied refreshments, meals or accommodation to workers, or perhaps rope for use in the building works, as the new railway ran just a few dozen yards in front of his premises.

In 1839 Glover brought a case of assault against coal-miner Samuel Savage, the hearing being held at Penkridge. The defendant and his friends had entered the inn about 2 pm and, after drinking a pint, Savage became abusive to the other customers. He then stood up, took off his coat and challenged anyone present to a fight.

Without warning he struck a man by the name of Carter, knocked him to the floor and jumped on him. At this point the landlord intervened, telling Savage that he wouldn't accept such behaviour on a Sunday (as if was acceptable at any other time!) and that he should leave the premises. Savage took exception to this and began pushing and shoving Glover around, telling him that he'd treat him in the same way as Carter. In the end, Glover managed to eject him but before long Savage was back, demanding more drink, which Glover naturally refused to give him. This time Savage put on the coat he had left behind and, along with his friends, finally left.

The matter didn't end there though as at about 11 pm Savage was back yet again. By this time Glover and his family had retired to bed but Savage stood outside hurling abuse and even tried to climb the window shutters to get to the first floor!

In his defence, Savage alleged that the present case had only been brought because *he* had taken out a warrant against Glover's nephew, Henry, a few weeks earlier. Either way, the evidence of Glover's servant and Savage's friends were completely contradictory and the case was therefore dismissed with each party left to meet its own costs.

The third case concerns a group of three men who had been drinking at the Black Lion one evening in December 1841. They set off for Wolverhampton at around eight o'clock but by the time they reached Oxley, a quarrel had broken out between two of them, Frederick Sambrook and Peter Perry. When the row came to blows, a group of bystanders intervened and suggested that the dispute be settled by a "proper" stand-up fight.

After a few rounds of this bare-knuckle contest Sambrook collapsed and his injuries were so bad that he died two days later. Perry and the third man, Beddesford, who had acted as his 'second' during the fight, were indicted on a charge of manslaughter.

At the trial in March the men offered no defence and were found guilty, although they each received a comparatively light one month sentence. The judge explained the reason for his leniency; nothing unfair had taken place during the fight and the men had already been incarcerated for three months while awaiting trial.

Glover was still running the Black Lion in 1851 but within a decade it had become a farm, initially worked by one Walter Aston. In the 1830s it was part of the Monckton estate but by 1920, the building at least, was in possession of the Bickford family - it may have been so since it was first built as they owned many properties in this area. Today 'Black Lion Farm' has purely residential use.[91]

The Golden Ball

The Golden Ball Inn, or just 'The Ball Inn' was a well known public house situated on the Wolverhampton to Stafford road. It stood very close to the present-day Ball Lane entrance to Coven Heath, on a patch of ground now used as a car park for the allotments.

Joseph Moseley, described as 'advanced in years', was landlord of the Ball at his death in 1831 and three years later, Thomas Spilsbury was the keeper.

In January 1847 a shooting competition to be held at The Ball was advertised in the regional press, the prize being a 'Fat Pig', with entrants charged £1 each. The event was open to anyone residing within 30 miles of Wolverhampton and there was a limit of one and a half ounces on the weight of shot. Presumably this was a target-shooting contest rather than trying to shoot the prize!

From at least 1846, the Golden Ball (and to a lesser extent the Four Ashes) was the venue for many 'Pedestrianism' events - walking races on which the participants put up money and spectators placed bets. These meetings were usually held at public houses that were out of town but easily accessible. They excited interest across the nation, being extensively reported in newspapers, and often drew very large crowds. A newspaper report of 1852 noted in relation to one contest that "the forthcoming event is the sole topic of conversation in the Black Country". Some races were short 'sprints' of 300 yards where others were two or more miles. Contestants and spectators would come to the Ball from all parts of the Midlands and further afield.

Figure 117: The Ball Inn during Frank Harding's tenure in the early 20th century

In 1850 Frederick Coates of Wednesfield and William Hill of Lye took part in a one mile race, each putting up a £10 stake. The over-confident Hill gave Coates a twenty yard start and lost the race as a result, managing to regain nothing of the advantage he had given away. The winning time was recorded as five minutes and two seconds and Coates collected his winnings at the inn during the evening. In 1856, a 300-yard race between Arthur Akers of Birmingham and Benjamin Badger of Wolverhampton was run for £40, equivalent to at least £3,000 today!

In the early 1850s, Richard Humpage was landlord of the Ball. Like many publicans he had another occupation, in this particular case, as a wheelwright. Ten years later, locally born Samuel Daw kept the Golden Ball assisted by his wife Eleanor, one servant and an 'Ostler', a man who looked after horses and stabling. Mr Daw was still licensee at his death in June 1878.

Eleanor Daw continued as landlady until 1882 when the lease of the inn was put up for auction in Birmingham. It was described as

Figure 118: The Golden Ball and adjacent filling station in the 1950s.

"one of the best in the midland counties" and "of great note". Three cottages and over four acres of land were also available if required. The pub was acquired by a Mr Riley who, before making extensive alterations, decided to auction off much of the contents. Up for sale were feather beds, mahogany furniture, clocks, engravings, casks, carts and harness, brewing equipment and many other trade items.

Five years later, in 1887, Benjamin Tranter was the landlord; he had invested in Hopyard Colliery at Bentley with his father in 1884 but poor trading conditions and flooding at the mine had forced him into bankruptcy. At a meeting of his creditors he tried to protect what assets he retained by claiming that the goods and chattels of the Golden Ball belonged to his wife!

By 1891 the Golden Ball was kept by Scotsman James Davidson Robb, although business could not have been good as two years earlier, he had unsuccessfully tried to dispose of his lease. The demise was advertised as a "roadside country inn" described as having "good brewing plant, stabling, piggeries and so forth; three acres of land; large garden". Robb subsequently moved to licensed premises at Burton Upon Trent.

Near the end of the nineteenth century a minor court case mentions a 'coconut alley' at Coven Heath. It does not say whether this was associated with the Ball or perhaps a travelling show pitched on the Heath.

In 1901 Thomas Chambers of Abbots Bromley was the landlord and he was followed in 1911 by George William Venables of Wolverhampton. Venables employed no servants, suggesting that the Inn was generally quieter than in previous years.

At some point in the early decades of the 20th century, Frank Henry Harding was the publican, as was H E Holloway - on one postcard of the Inn at this time, it is described as "The famous calling house". From at least 1908 until the outbreak of the First World War, Henry Hudson was the keeper.

In the twentieth century, as horse drawn traffic declined with the arrival of the combustion engine, a garage came into being beside the Ball, offering fuel for sale from a single row of roadside pumps. For the latter part of its existence the Golden Ball was in the hands of Mitchell & Butlers brewery.[92]

The New Inn

The New Inn, in Coven village, was a public house for about forty years before becoming a shop. It seems to have changed hands quite frequently and probably incorporated some form of shop from its earliest days.

In 1860 John Brookes was the keeper of the New Inn. At a court case early in that year, a man named Quinton was charged with obtaining a total of six barrels of beer by deception and having them delivered to the New Inn, where they were sold. Whether Brookes was in some way complicit in the affair is not known; the case against Quinton was dismissed and the brewers who had lost out were advised to take a civil action against him to recover their losses.

In spring 1861 Daniel Oakley (or Oakey) of Derbyshire was the landlord but in the same year he was also listed in the Harrison, Harrod Directory and Gazetteer of Staffordshire as a shopkeeper.

Over the next twenty years there were at least three different keepers; Ann Wright, Thomas Hill and Elizabeth Vaughan.

On New Years Eve 1888, a 16-year-old servant at the inn, Phoebe Challinor, took a set of keys from Mrs Vaughan's daughter. When quizzed about the keys a few days later, the girl admitted taking them and handed them back. Nothing more was thought of the matter until it was discovered that a whole ham was missing. When questioned, a boy who was also employed at the Inn, said that he had seen Challinor with the missing meat. The young woman was charged with the theft, tried at the Stafford Quarter Sessions and found guilty. She received a sentence of one month imprisonment with hard labour at Stafford Gaol.

Mrs Vaughan seems to have had enough of the business by July of that year, as the New Inn was advertised to let with immediate possession by Springfield Brewery. It was described as a fully-licensed Country House with stabling for eight horses, a coach house and a good garden.

By 1896 the transformation of the New Inn from public house to shop was definitely under-way, as Martha Bickley, who had been there for some five years was described in local directories as 'landlady and shopkeeper'. Her husband Thomas was a bookmaker.

At some point before 1902 the premises ceased to be a pub altogether and within a short while became 'Wiggins Stores' and, a little later, the village bakery.[93]

The Rainbow

Three cottages stood on the site of the Rainbow in 1777 and at some time before 1819 they were either replaced with, or converted to, a public house.

One of the earliest landlords of the Rainbow was James Yates, who kept the inn during the 1830s. At this time there was a rival 'beer-house' in the village kept by one James Hughes. Following an 1830 Act of Parliament, anyone could obtain a license to brew and sell beer and, as a result, many such beer-houses had come into being. They were run by individuals, quite literally selling beer from their front rooms and, as can be imagined, nearby inns and taverns were often unhappy with this free-for-all situation. The only advantage that 'licensed victuallers' had over the beer-houses was that they could sell spirits, although they no doubt offered better facilities and more convivial surroundings!

By 1851 William Hughes, possibly related to the aforementioned James, was in charge at the Rainbow and it was towards the end of his tenure that the tension between beer-house and licensed premises in Coven came to a head. A case at the Wolverhampton Police Court in June 1859 heard that the village had been the scene of outrages of a type "only to be experienced in Ireland"!

At this time John Brookes ran a beer-house almost opposite the Rainbow and had himself applied for a spirit license. According to Brookes, the prospect of another full-blown competitor on their doorstep had spurred those with a vested interest in the Rainbow to try to sully his reputation and thereby prevent a license being issued. Somewhat surprisingly it seems that John Smith, farmer, landowner and friend of the Methodist chapel was one of the chief instigators of this minor conspiracy.

The story begins on the night of 15th May when someone fired two shots through the bedroom window of John Hadderley, who lived in one of the cottages opposite the 'Rainbow'. According to Hadderley, the shots came from the direction of Brookes' garden. In court he said that Brookes' house had been disorderly and that he lived in fear of the man, although he had never been threatened by him or even spoken to him.

Handbills were issued from the Chief Constable's office at Stafford two days after the shots were fired, offering a £5 reward for information regarding the person or persons responsible.

Some days later, James Milligan, an Irish labourer who worked for Brookes, was drinking at the Rainbow. With his tongue loosened by drink, he openly declared that it was Brookes who had fired the shots.

Once word of this got back to Brookes he became enraged and confronted Milligan while he was with William Jones, milking the cows at Grange Farm, at that time run by the Cliffts. He asked Milligan what he had been saying about him at the Rainbow and when Milligan replied "not much", Brookes grabbed him by the collar and hit him. He proceeded to drag Milligan out of the cow shed and threw him into a pond where he hit him again. Ann Clifft managed to pull Brookes off before he could beat Milligan further and she deposed in court that Brookes had said that it was a good job she was present or he would have killed him.

When he had calmed down and had time to reflect on his actions, Brookes felt that he had used too much violence. He gave Milligan money in compensation for the assault and, at the time, Milligan appeared to be satisfied with this arrangement. Nevertheless, it was Milligan, in name at least, who now brought Brookes to court. During the hearing it emerged that John Smith was the owner of the Rainbow and had supplied Milligan with the half-crown required to issue the summons. As Milligan did not appear in person to pursue the matter, Brookes' defence claimed that the case could not continue.

Someone must have been intimidating Brookes before the shooting incident, as another witness, local labourer's wife Emma Spicer, told the court she had been at Brookes' house and heard him say that some near neighbour intended to do him serious harm. Brookes said that if he found out who it was he would 'stick his pig' or burn down his house.

Brookes was fined 20 shillings plus costs for the assault and bound over to keep the peace towards Hadderley for six months on penalty of a £40 fine.

The attempt to prevent Brookes obtaining a license does not seem to have worked as by the following year he was running the New Inn but, as mentioned above, there was a question about his involvement in a case of obtaining goods by deception. In any event, Brookes was declared bankrupt before the end of 1860, being described as "having been out of work and latterly living in lodgings at Oxley Street, Wolverhampton".

According to a notice in the London Gazette, Brookes had been a journeyman miller at Standeford and also a dealer in cows and

Figure 119: The Rainbow around 1910. (M. Nicholls)

Figure 120: Offering Holt's beer, a bowling green and 'pleasure gardens' in the 1920s. (M. Nicholls)

pigs. He moved into Coven village and became a grocer, licensed brewer and retailer of beer and tobacco and continued to deal in livestock but soon went out of business.

Whether Brookes was simply unfortunate or whether he became a trouble-maker after earlier misfortune is difficult to ascertain, but his wife had died tragically in 1855. She had stooped down before the grate at their home in Shelsley, Worcestershire, and her clothes had caught fire. The accident caused premature delivery of their baby and she died as a result of her injuries about a month later.

It is interesting to note that Thomas, Ann Clifft's husband, was himself a beer-house keeper in 1851. The grave of Thomas and Ann Clifft can be seen in St Paul's churchyard.

William Hughes left the Rainbow in 1861, when it was taken over by Rutland-born Joseph Wells. Wells, who died in June 1876 and is also buried at St Paul's, was succeeded by Joseph Jackson of Bilston.

In 1883 Jackson was charged with allowing gaming on his premises. It was alleged that he and three customers, Hartshorn, Leviton and Hibbs played bagatelle for a quart of ale. As bagatelle was a game of chance it was illegal to play it for money, although it was common at the time (but nevertheless still illegal) for games to be played for 'checks' - tokens that could be spent at the public house concerned - and this is what Jackson claimed had happened.

Although four similar cases had been brought against Jackson in the past, the court decided that he had acted in ignorance of the law rather than with disregard for it. His license was not endorsed but he faced a fine and costs of over £2 in total.

Two weeks before the theft of a ham from the New Inn mentioned earlier, Joseph Tomkys, who had replaced Jackson as landlord at the Rainbow, received an evening visit from the police. Sergeant Titterton and two constables found local farmer Richard Oakley to be so drunk that he fell over when he stepped outside. Oakley, who was in his mid-fifties, was charged with drunkenness and Tomkys with permitting the same on his premises.

Oakley, who farmed at The Laches, told the court that he had only had three glasses of whiskey and that his condition was due to illness rather than drink; the magistrate was unconvinced and handed out a ten shilling fine. Tomkys was fined two pounds but his license was not endorsed and he remained as landlord for some years afterwards. The court case was attended by a Mr Harper, who was the owner of the Rainbow at that time, and like Tomkys, a Bilston man.

Tomkys lived in one of the cottages near the Rainbow after he retired and one of his neighbours also had a brush with the law. Roseanna Thacker, a girl who lived with her mother, found herself in court at Preston, Lancashire, on a charge of theft. She had left home to work 'in service' for at family at Blackpool, at the age of 15. For reasons unknown, and unbeknown to her mother, she ended up out of work and in the care of the Girls Friendly Society. From there she was taken into service by a Mr Thexton, from whom the theft was committed.

She had left Mr Thextons house without notice and was apprehended some time later carrying a watch and chain, a fur boa and a pair of boots, all belonging to her employer. Roseanna's mother, Mary, travelled to Preston to plead for her in court and it seems that the young woman was truly remorseful. She was spared a prison sentence provided that she agreed to go home with her mother and paid a ten shilling fine.

In 1896, and until after the turn of the century, Tom Rodhouse was the publican but by the start of the Great War it was in the hands of William Baker.

There was a slaughterhouse at the rear of the Rainbow in the early part of the twentieth century, operated by the landlord. At this time the pub was part of Manchester-based Holts Brewery but in 1927 Ansells took over the establishment.

Like many pubs and larger private houses, the Rainbow at one time had its own bowling green but the sport, in one form or another, had been carried on in the village for a considerable time. When William Woolridge died in 1774, his will specified that three annuities from Bowling Alley Piece should be distributed among the poor of Coven, Brewood and Standeford and this income continued until at least the middle of the twentieth century. Bowling Alley

Piece is the field adjacent to the waterworks track at Standeford Green. Bowling *Green* Piece was the name of the square field behind Grange Farm on the opposite side of the alley to the Rainbow.

In common with other public houses of the time, the pub served as a base for sports and recreational groups. It had its own football team for most of the last century and was at one time home to the Rainbow Horticultural Club. Formed in the mid-50s, the club held shows there every Sunday morning during the summer months.

The old Rainbow stood until 1968 but its replacement was burned down before completion and required reconstruction.[94]

Four Ashes Inn

In the 1700s, the important stagecoach routes to and from London were gradually put under the control of turnpike trusts, who were able to charge tolls and with the money so raised, maintain and improve the roads they controlled. The road from Wolverhampton to Stafford, being a part of the London to Liverpool route, was turnpiked in 1760 and the Four Ashes Inn may have been built specifically to serve the increased traffic along the Stafford Road; it certainly existed by 1775 and probably gave its name to the small hamlet that gradually grew up around it.

Samuel Ward was one of the earliest keepers of the Four Ashes and he also worked as a gamekeeper for Edward Monckton. The inn is said to have been gifted to the family after Samuel's son Joseph, who was also a gamekeeper on the Somerford Estate, saved a member of the Monckton family from drowning. The inn passed from Joseph to his sister Jane, then to his brother Samuel, a man who is said to have witnessed the first and last mail coaches to stop at the Four Ashes. Jane married David Kirk, a mail coach driver, the couple no doubt having met at the inn. David Kirk died prematurely at the age of 38, after falling ill while on a trip to Liverpool in 1827.

The Four Ashes was the venue for an auction in 1819, when the stock of Walsall timber merchant Joseph Barker went under the

Figure 121: Jugs carrying the names of Joseph Ward, 1799 and David Kirk, 1826. (M.Robinson)

hammer. Whether Barker had gone bust or had died the auction notice does not say. We may wonder why the sale was held so far from Walsall; the most likely reason is that being a stop on the turnpike would allow potential buyers from far and wide to visit and, importantly, ship away goods via the nearby canal - this was, after all, before the start of the railway era. In December 1830, in another typical auction, the possessions of one William Tristram, a Willenhall butcher, were sold at the Four Ashes. Once again, the auction was advertised in newspapers circulating far from the area, and this was still before the arrival of the railway.

Mogg's railway guide of 1840 tells how the Four Ashes pub was frequented by the mail-coaches returning from Liverpool in earlier days, although some coaches were still operating when the guide was published. At this time there was another track running in a south-easterly direction from the crossroads at Four Ashes, although it may have only served to permit access to fields. The direction of this track of this can be seen from the alignment of the house now known as 'Fifth Ash'. The triangular field, now wooded, between the track and the Stafford Road was known as 'Roundabout'.

Jane Kirk continued to live at the Four Ashes with her children and brothers until she passed away in 1843. When Samuel died in 1859, the inn passed to Jane's son Samuel Martin Kirk, who ran the inn for more than thirty years. It was he who put up the little verse, telling customers that there was no credit or 'tab' available:

> "I strive to keep a decent tap
> For ready money but no strap"

The graves of several of the Kirk family from this era can be seen on the east side of St Mary & St Chad, Brewood.

There was a constant stream of people passing the inn during one day and night in 1856 - they were amongst the thousands gathering at Stafford to witness the execution of the infamous Rugeley poisoner, Dr Palmer. A single passer-by a few years later was just as interesting - a man who undertook to walk the entire distance from Wolverhampton to Stafford on a ball! These and many other stories about local characters and incidents have been passed down through generations of the Kirk family.

Samuel Martin Kirk's son Edwin married Annie Elizabeth Yeomans and the couple lived at Four Ashes farm, near the canal bridge, before running the pub. Edwin was keen on breeding and showing poultry; in 1886 for example, he won a five shilling prize for his Spanish hen at the Northamptonshire Show. It was he who built a stable beside the inn, which was later converted to serve as the lounge bar, and allowed the erection of a 'Buxton and Bonnet' advertising sign in exchange for a new suit each year! Their son Sidney went on to become a very successful farmer at Brewood Park Farm.

The Albrighton Hunt, was due to play host to a very important visitor at the Four Ashes on Monday 14th March 1881. Her Imperial Highness, the Empress of Austria, was on a hunting tour of the country and was expected to join Lord Wrottesley, Sir Thomas Oughey and others at the meeting. She withdrew from the event as a mark of respect, following the assassination of the Emperor of Russia, Alexander II, on the previous day.

In 1899 a syndicate conducted speculative boring operations near the Four Ashes and managed to locate a three-foot thick coal

Figure 122: Samuel Martin Kirk, keeper of the Four Ashes for around thirty years in the second half of the 19th century. (K.Robinson)

Figure 123: Edwin Kirk and his daughter at Four Ashes Farm, 1900. (K.Robinson)

Figure 124: The Albrighton Hunt assembled at the Four Ashes Inn. (L. Dutton)

Figure 125: The Four Ashes in 1926, showing old and new forms of transport and the 'Buxton and Bonnet' sign at far left. (L. Dutton)

> **SUPERIOR TRAVELLING AT REDUCED FARES,**
> BY A NEW DIRECT DAY COACH TO CHESTER AND LI-VERPOOL.
>
> THE ZEPHYR, an elegant, well-appointed, light, Safety Coach, is dispatched every morning, except Monday, at eight o'clock, from the NELSON HOTEL, Coach-office, Birmingham, in nine hours and a half, to the ANGEL HOTEL and Saddle Coach-office, Dale-street, Liverpool.
>
> ROUTE,
>
> Through Westbromwich, Wednesbury, Bilston, Wolverhampton, Coven, Brewood, Invetsy Bank, Newport, Fernhill, Sandford, Whitchurch, Market Drayton, Malpas, Broxton, and Chester.
>
> RADENHURST and Co., Proprietors.
>
> The above coach has been appointed at the solicitations of the gentry and trading community, who have lately been considerably inconvenienced in consequence of the want of the accommodation that this conveyance will afford. The Proprietors pledge themselves that it shall be conducted, in all its appointments, in an approved style, and are determined that it shall not be surpassed by any other conveyance; and confidently rely upon receiving that support from the public that their exertions may be considered to merit.

Figure 126: An advertisement for 'The Zephyr' in the Birmingham Journal 1838. The coach offered a swift nine and a half hour journey to Liverpool!

Figure 127: Members of the Kirk family in front of the inn around the time of the First World War. (K.Robinson)

seam, extending from the direction of the Cannock coal fields although nothing more seems to have come of it. An area south-east of the canal bridge at Four Ashes, where a new incinerator plant has recently been built, was a sand and gravel quarry until the 1950s.

When her husband died in 1910, Annie Elizabeth Kirk took over the running of the Four Ashes. She seems to have been a capable landlady, although in 1920 she was fined for overcharging for rum following a visit by 'Weights and Measures' inspectors. Despite the drink being well above the minimum *strength* required by law, she had technically served a short measure. Had the inspectors called on the following day, when new rules came into force, the case would not have arisen. A fine and costs totalling more than five pounds were imposed.

At one time the pub had a garden and orchard at the rear, and what is now a small car park opposite, was its front garden. Around the end of the nineteenth century, an old cottage which stood where the main car park now lies, was home to the four Bowdler sisters and their considerable collection of 18 cats! Before the establishment of the industrial estate, the area around Four Ashes was said to be a very pleasant place for walking. People would come to walk along the canal or in Somerford Woods and the inn catered for these visitors with an upstairs refreshment room in addition to the bar.

The road now known as Station Drive did not run as far as Watling Street in the early part of the 19th century; instead it terminated upon Calf Heath, as did the Straight Mile. Although the approach to Four Ashes station was tree-lined, the woodland now on the south side of the road did not come into being until the second half of the 20th century. This woodland stands on 'Four Ashes Pit', a Site of Special Scientific Interest, containing material laid down in the last ice age.[95]

Harrow Inn

On a fine, moonlit night in November 1830, the Birmingham to Liverpool mail-coach, drawn by four horses and with lamps blazing, thundered past Coven along the narrow Stafford Road. As it approached Standeford Bridge, the coachman saw a 'car', a light two-wheeler, approaching at a furious pace. He shouted his usual warning "halloo" but it was ignored by the two men in the oncoming vehicle, both of whom were completely intoxicated. The vehicles met in a head-on collision and the shaft of the car pierced the chest of one of the leading horses of the mail-coach.

The driver of the car suffered a head injury but his passenger escaped unscathed. The coachman tried to raise the landlord of 'The Harrow' for assistance but he refused to get up! The poor horse was gushing blood from its wound whenever it moved and, having no means to end its suffering, the coachman had little choice but to leave it to die at the roadside and continue on to Penkridge with the remaining three horses. The unhelpful landlord in this episode was most probably William Pearson who ran the pub for the first half of this decade.

At the end of the '30s Thomas Buckley was the keeper of The Harrow and two fields beside the brook at the rear of the pub, known as 'Standeford Field' and 'Little Croft'. Ten years later William Buckley, perhaps a relative, was the licensee. John Walker

Cartwright, an ex-publican was also living at Standeford at this time. In 1875 the Harrow and the Anchor Inn were both owned by the Bickford family.

There must have been a concerted effort by police to stamp out illegal gaming in the area in 1883. In the same month that the landlord of the Rainbow was charged with allowing betting on games of bagatelle, William Shemilt of the Harrows was summonsed but this time the game was target shooting at a candle. Shemilt, it was alleged, had put up a prize of half a gallon of ale and the shooting match was to be followed by tossing coins for additional drinks. The contest took place at eleven in the morning but Shemilt claimed in court that the men involved had 'got him up out of spite' to host the match, although he freely admitted to providing the gun!

Shemilt's wife claimed that the contest was for amusement, not for drink, and she denied that any coin-tossing had taken place. Barmaid Maria Adams corroborated her employer's version of events and claimed that two of the men, the Stanton brothers, had been very abusive towards Shemilt and his wife. She also said that they had paid for drink afterwards, not had it as a prize. As there was doubt about who was telling the truth, the court decided that a fine of just over one pound was sufficient.

Shemilt appeared as a witness in a case of trespass brought at the Penkridge Petty Sessions in 1884. The matter concerned shooting rights on land belonging to Richard Oakley of The Laches and George Thompson of Aspley Farm, and whether a particular hare had been shot in one place or another. In that same year Shemilt, who was described as a victualler and farmer, was declared bankrupt, with assets of £44 against liabilities of £203.

In 1888 Constables Lawton and Horn took in William Hodgkins for being drunk and disorderly at the Harrow. Penkridge Police Court handed out a fine and costs of over 12 shillings - the price of around seventy pints of beer at the prevailing twopence a pint.

In 1891 locally-born William Waring was the licensee and The Harrow, along with the Rainbow and the Anchor, was granted a music license in 1892. The premises were put up for sale the following year, being advertised with "six acres of turf and trout fishing"

Figure 128: The Harrows in 1926, when a drinks shelf either side of the front door added to the list of outdoor amenities! (L. Dutton)

Figure 129: Bowling green beside the The Harrows and, in the background, an exceptionally tall telegraph pole.

in the adjacent Saredon Brook. Edwin Tranter seems to have taken over for the remaining years of the century until Yorkshire-born Simpson Bowes took the license.

A decade later, Robert Latham was in charge but when he applied for renewal of his license at 'The Harrows' (no longer called 'The Harrow') in 1914, there was an objection due to a recent conviction. In that case, Mr Latham had been fined 40 shillings for selling out of hours on a Sunday morning. The court that heard the earlier case were told that Latham was upstairs getting dressed when a member of his household had admitted and served fifteen men, about a dozen of whom were miners 'out for a drive'.

Latham came to the renewal hearing at the Penkridge Licensing Sessions well prepared; the brewery said that it would be difficult to find a more reliable man, and he even had the support of Reverend Forrester (then at Cannock), who provided a testimonial stating that the house had always been well conducted and that Mr and Mrs Latham were worthy of a position of trust. The vicar wished it to be known that he had not visited The Harrows as a customer however, simply in relation to parochial matters! The license was duly renewed.

The Harrows was a meeting place for the Albrighton Hunt in the first three decades of the new century, as was the Four Ashes. It also had a bowling green, where the car park is now located, and its own football team from at least 1910.[96]

The Anchor

The Anchor lies so close to the Staffordshire and Worcestershire Canal that anglers were once said to fish from inside the pub, casting their lines through the windows! In addition to moorings, the Anchor had two cottages and stabling at the northern end of the yard. Horses employed on the canal were a fundamental part of any boat-owner's business and they had to be well looked after.

In the 1830s John Durham was the landlord but by 1840 it had passed to Thomas Hammersley, who had an exceptionally long

Figure 130: The Anchor Inn and buildings behind in 1907.

tenure; he was in charge for at least thirty years and was almost eighty by the time his stint came to an end! At the start of Mr Hammersley's occupancy, the land on which the pub and canal wharf stood was owned by William Bickford.

Like all pubs, The Anchor had brushes with the law involving both customers and landlords. A newspaper report of 1880 tells how the landlord, "Thomas Hartshorn" (probably William Hartshorn who was the inn-keeper at that time) was summonsed on a charge of assaulting a Darlaston man, Enoch Firm.

The attack happened following a fatal accident in the vicinity, late one Saturday night. A group of Darlaston men were returning through Coven in a horse and trap when it collided with another vehicle. Almost all the occupants of the trap were pitched into the road and one, a man of about seventy named Jeremiah Downes, died almost immediately as a result of his injuries. Hartshorn was at the scene and tried to drive away. When Firm grabbed Hartshorn's horse by the head to try and stop him, Hartshorn struck the man in the face, giving him a black eye. Hartshorn was fined twenty shillings plus costs for the assault. Whether he was in some way responsible for the crash is not known.

Hartshorn had left before the end of the decade, by which time a Mr Cope was in charge. At about three in the afternoon of Thursday 10th October 1889, one William Shenton went in to the Anchor bar and tried to buy a pint of ale. As he was already completely inebriated, the landlord's daughter, Alice, refused to serve him. Annoyed at this refusal, Shenton left the pub and began making a disturbance around Cross Green but he was soon apprehended by constable Maguire. This disorderly conduct landed Shenton in court where a fine and costs totalling just under a pound were imposed.

A charge of permitting drunkenness on his premises was brought against Alfred Walker, who was the landlord in early 1900. A man named Wakefield was seen by PC Poulton to enter the Anchor, quite sober, at about 12:30 in the afternoon, and emerge in a drunken state around 3 o'clock. Walker told the constable that he had served Wakefield with very little drink and had asked him to leave.

Wakefield, who was obviously a friend of Walker, was called as a witness by the defence and said that although he had asked for a pint of ale, Walker had refused to serve him and told him to go away, although he remained in the house with a group of men. The case was dismissed as there was doubt as to whether Wakefield had been served when drunk.

Edwin Scattergood was the landlord in the years leading up to the Great War and he appeared as a witness in a case of theft tried at Penkridge in 1913. Two men of no fixed abode, who had done some work for him at the Anchor, were charged with stealing fifteen ounces of tobacco. They were also charged with theft of tools, a clock and a bicycle pump (!) while working at Wheaton Aston. The pair pleaded guilty to the pilfering and were given prison sentences with hard labour.

The old Anchor Inn was demolished in the 1960s, and like the Rainbow, the new building has been refurbished several times since.[97]

Figure 131: A 1930s view taken from Cross Green. (M. Nicholls)

Figure 132: The old Anchor Inn, about ten years before it was demolished. (M. Nicholls)

Appendix 1

The following is a list of names found on most of the older graves in St Paul's churchyard. They are grouped by surname but the individuals so listed may not be related. A photographic archive of the monumental inscriptions is available from the author via the publisher's email address.

    Cartwright John Walker
    Griffiths Sarah
    Jackson Thomas, Mary
    Shotton Elizabeth, James, Sarah, Benjamin
    Wright James, Thomas Henry
    Lovatt Thomas, Sarah
    Jarvis Elizabeth, James
    Partridge Mary, William
    Alcock Emma, Edwin, Ann
    Wood Annie Elizabeth, Sarah
    Reynolds William Walford, Letitia, Sarah
    Childe George
    Wootton Frank T(a)leepee, Jonah, Mary
    Pullen Edward, Richard
    Clifft Thomas, Ann
    Ward Edward, Jane
    Phillips Edward, Sarah
    Dawkes Henry, Fanny Louisa, Henry
    Foster Simeon, Prudence
    Austin John Shenstone
    Hughes Dorothy, Mary Ann Issard

Baker Sarah, George
Jackson William, Harriet, Eliza, Robert, Jane
Dodd Robert, Eliza
Plant John, Sarah
Hall William
Bowdler Richard, Sarah, Hannah
Baker George
Yeomans Moses
George Catherine, John, Fanny Louisa
Buckley Eliza, John
Edwards Joseph, Hannah, Charles
Coleclough Constance Mary, Frederick
Price Harriet, John
Phillips Martha, Silvester
Hughes Ann, Albert
Perkins Mary, Henry
Raison Elizabeth, John
Southall William, Emily
Bishton Benjamin William
Wells Joseph
Perkin James
Roberts Edward, Ellen
Lewis Ida May
Reeves Mary, Joseph
French Lizzie, Rosina, Samuel Coombes
Williams John Thomas, Miriam Mabel
Hadley Winifred, Charles, William
Whittingham Henry, William, Maria
Thomas George, Martha
Southall Lilian, Charles T, Harriet
Davies George, Eliza

Appendix 2

Roll Of Honour

1914 - 1918

Edwin Wellings	December 1914
James Snead	May 1916
Charles Hayward	July 1916
William Jones	August 1917
Bert Davis	September 1917
Victor Upperdine	September 1917
Joseph Deans	September 1917
R S Pullen	October 1917
Charles Bickley	March 1918
Frank Highway	April 1918
W Wellings	June 1918
George H Davis	October 1918
Alfred Morris	November 1918

1939 - 1945

George H Ward	March 1941
Thomas E Smith	November 1941
Kenneth W Pringle	January 1944
John D Vincent	June 1944
James H Sayfritz	July 1944
E A Cooke	September 1944
David Muir	May 1945

Notes

1. Staffordshire Advertiser 30th June 1832, Ordnance Survey 1834, Lichfield Mercury 27th May 1932
2. Manchester Courier and Lancashire General Advertiser 5th August 1876, Dover Express 14th July 1899
3. Staffordshire Advertiser 5th October 1839, Lichfield Mercury 14th May 1909
4. Staffordshire Advertiser 21st March 1835
5. National Archives MS3810/99, Whites Directory 1834, Harrison, Harrod Directory & Gazetteer of Staffordshire 1861, Kelly's Directory 1896, Ordnance Survey Map 1902, 1911 Census RG14PN16925 SD1 ED11 SN96, David Horovitz 'Some notes on the history of Brewood p292
6. Notes & Collection Relating To Brewood 1860, Staffordshire Advertiser 12th June 1802, Birmingham Daily Post 11th April 1900
7. Tithe Map, Whites Directory 1834, Whites Directory 1851, Memoirs of Victor Francis
8. 1861 census RG09 piece 1981 folio 12 page 17
9. London Gazette 9th November 1888
10. Parish registers St Georges Wolverhampton 1824 and 1839, Coventry Herald 27th November 1835, Post Office Directory of Birmingham Staffordshire & Worcestershire 1850, Whites Directory 1851, Register of Births Marriages and Deaths Sep 1882 Shoolbred William 87 Wolverhampton 6b 281
11. H M Whitehead map of 1927
12. Staffordshire Advertiser 6th November 1830
13. London Gazette 1st September 1899
14. Wolverhampton Archives & Local Studies Probate Date 22nd January 1866
15. DB-44/2/1/12 etc Wolverhampton Archives & Local Studies, Staffordshire Advertiser 30th January 1802
16. Whites Commercial Directory, General & Commercial Directory 1818, Birmingham Gazette 10th February 1834, Birmingham Daily Gazette 22nd May 1868, Edinburgh Evening News 25 November 1933
17. Brewood Tithe Map, London Gazette 2nd May 1899, London Gazette 21st September 1900
18. Staffordshire Advertiser 4th March 1797, Whites Directory 1851, An historical and descriptive account of the collegiate church of Wolverhampton 1836
19. Aberdeen Journal 21st June 1898
20. Wolverhampton Archives DB-44/2/1/1, Whites Commercial Directory 1851, Birmingham Gazette 27th May 1876
21. Western Times 6th November 1868
22. Lichfield Mercury 21st September 1900, Birmingham Daily Post 31st December 1895, Sussex Agricultural Express 4th August 1899, Western Morning News 4th February 1949, Brewood Park Farm sale particulars 1918

23. William Salt Library M199/2 etc, Wolverhampton Archives Ref DB-44/2, 'A Survey of the Manor of Coven' c.1800

24. Morning Post 4th September 1845, Register of Births, Marriages and Deaths Sep 1845 HEATH William Penkridge 17 68, Staffordshire Advertiser 31th August 1839, Cheltenham Chronicle 23rd April 1904, Birmingham Gazette 5th December 1914, Illustrated Police News 1st July 1882, 1891 Census RG12 Piece Number 2233 Folio 126 Page 3, Grantham Journal 17th December 1898, Board of Trade Accident Report 22nd February 1855, London Standard 15th March 1875, Tamworth Herald 6th March 1880, Gloucester Citizen 16th June 1893, Dundee Courier 18th October 1907, Western Daily Press 18th October 1907

25. Birmingham Journal 24th August 1867

26. London Gazette 21st November 1873, London Gazette 20th November 1874, London Gazette 1st July 1879

27. Nottinghamshire Guardian 23rd December 1858, Lichfield Mercury 14th August 1896, Lichfield Mercury 16th October 1908, William Pitt 'A Topographical History of Staffordshire'

28. The History of South Staffordshire Waterworks Company 1853-1989 by Johann Van Leerzem and Brian Williams, SSW archives

29. Staffordshire Advertiser 23rd October 1830

30. D3186/1 Staff & Worcs Canal plan 1770

31. Victoria County History

32. Staffordshire Advertiser 13th February 1847, Whites Directory 1851, Birmingham Daily Post 27th September 1859, Birmingham Daily Post 24th April 1861, Birmingham Daily Post 30th July 1872, Lichfield Mercury 29th august 1884, Lichfield Mercury 17th April 1885, Hampshire Telegraph 31st March 1888, Hampshire Telegraph 24th May 1890, Hampshire Telegraph 29th October 1892, Hampshire Telegraph 3rd September 1892

33. Register of Births, Marriages and Deaths: 1851 Brooke Elizabeth Penkridge 17 91, 1854 Chorlton 8c 572, 1910 Wandsworth 1d 279

34. Birmingham Gazette 4th April 1853, London Gazette 25th March 1853, Post Office Directory of Birmingham Staffordshire & Worcestershire 1850, Lancaster Gazette 30th January 1858, Staffordshire Sentinel 27th September 1856, Birmingham Journal 25th September 1858, London Gazette 20th August 1858, Chester Chronicle 29th September 1860, London Gazette 5th April 1861, Birmingham Daily Post 19th September 1861, Hereford Times 11 January 1862, Staffordshire Sentinel and Commercial & General Advertiser 26th September 1863, Information from Ray Shill, Birmingham Daily Post 15th November 1862, Birmingham Daily Gazette 24 September 1862, Perry's Bankrupt Gazette 2nd April 1864, Birmingham Daily Post 26th April 1864, Birmingham Daily Post 15th March 1870, 1871 Census RG10 piece 2923 folio 13 page 8, London Standard 20th January 1875, Birmingham Daily Post 1st July 1882, South Staffs Historic Environment Assessment appendix 2

35. 1891 census RG12 piece 2218 folio 44 page 3, 1901 census RG13 piece 2661

folio 36 page 3, 1851 census HO107 piece 2016 folio 333 page 14/15, 1861 census RG09 piece 1981 folio 25 page 4, Birmingham Daily Post 24th December 1870, Staffordshire Advertiser 30th January 1836, Staffordshire Advertiser 28th April 1838, Nottingham Evening Post 29th January 1894, 'The Model Locomotive Engineer, Fireman and Engine-boy', Coven Methodist Church Centenary Celebrations brochure 1939

36. Staffordshire Advertiser 10th April 1802
37. Birmingham Daily Post 23rd May 1884
38. Lichfield Mercury 31st July 1896
39. Lichfield Mercury 6th March 1908
40. Lichfield Mercury 22nd October 1909
41. Birmingham Daily Post 9th April 1866
42. Staffordshire Sentinel and Commercial & General Advertiser 22nd January 1870, Tamworth Herald 15th April 1882, Gloucester Citizen 20th March 1926
43. Lichfield Mercury 7th July 1899
44. Birmingham Gazette 2nd December 1876, Morpeth Herald 7th December 1878, Stafford Quarter Sessions April 1797, Hicks Smith - Brewood: a resume historical and topographical 1874
45. Lichfield Mercury 25th August 1911
46. Lichfield Mercury 31st August 1900
47. Staffordshire Advertiser 1st September 1838, Staffordshire Advertiser 26th June 1847, Lichfield Mercury 9th November 1883, Lichfield Mercury 28 March 1884, Lichfield Mercury 10th October 1884, Lichfield Mercury 9th January 1885, Lichfield Mercury 23rd March 1888
48. Lichfield Mercury 13th September 1895, The Times 30th October 1895
49. Lichfield Mercury 18th October 1912, Lichfield Mercury 29th November 1912, Lichfield Mercury 25th July 1913, Lichfield Mercury 8th September 1899, Lichfield Mercury 9th September 1921, Lichfield Mercury 21st May 1915, Lichfield Mercury 26th May 1916
50. Staffordshire Advertiser 29th October 1831
51. Lichfield Mercury 7th September 1900
52. Birmingham Daily Post 13th April 1886
53. Lichfield Mercury 26th August 1910
54. Birmingham Daily Post 16th August 1880
55. Lichfield Mercury 31st August 1883
56. Manchester Courier and Lancashire General Advertiser 14th June 1907, Manchester Courier and Lancashire General Advertiser 21st February 1908
57. Western Morning News 1st December 1922, Hull Daily Mail 1st December 1922, Hartlepool Mail 2nd December 1922, Yorkshire Post and Leeds Intelligencer 4th December 1922, Register of Births Marriages & Deaths Dec 1922 Cadwallader, Pauline M, 19, Cannock 6b 483, The History of the Kirk Family by Nora M Kirk

58. Manchester Courier and Lancashire General Advertiser 28th June 1884, Birmingham Daily Post 30th June 1884, Lichfield Mercury 4th July 1884
59. Lichfield Mercury 26th January 1900
60. Lichfield Mercury 9th November 1894
61. Lichfield Mercury 5th July 1895
62. Lichfield Mercury 12th January 1900
63. Lichfield Mercury 9th January 1914
64. Lichfield Mercury 5th September 1902
65. Birmingham Daily Post 16th December 1890
66. Lichfield Mercury 3rd June 1904
67. Evening Despatch 19th June 1914, Hitchmough's Black Country Pubs, The History of the Kirk Family by Nora M Kirk
68. Birmingham Daily Post 9th May 1890
69. Lichfield Mercury 26th October 1894, Birmingham Daily Post 23rd July 1889
70. Lichfield Mercury 10th February 1911
71. Lichfield Mercury 25th July 1913
72. Lichfield Mercury 18th June 1909
73. Birmingham Gazette 18th November 1876
74. Staffordshire Advertiser 1st December 1804
75. Staffordshire Advertiser 8th May 1830
76. The Natural History of Staffordshire, Robert Plot
77. The Birmingham Daily Mail 4th June 1883
78. Lichfield Mercury 8th October 1909
79. Lichfield Mercury 23rd February 1912, Lichfield Mercury 10th January 1913, Lichfield Mercury 5th February 1915, Lichfield Mercury 7th April 1922
80. Cheltenham Chronicle 2nd June 1906
81. Aldershot Military Gazette 12th September 1868
82. Berkshire Chronicle 24th November 1827
83. Staffordshire Sentinel and Commercial & General Advertiser 25th January 1879
84. Birmingham Daily Post 16th January 1883
85. Stafford Quarter Sessions 1777-1839
86. Lichfield Mercury 8th November 1889
87. Stafford Quarter Sessions 1777-1839
88. Lichfield Mercury 28th January 1921
89. Lichfield Mercury 31st March 1893
90. Birmingham Daily Post 11th November 1891
91. Staffordshire Advertiser 10th June 1837, Staffordshire Advertiser 8th July 1837, Staffordshire Advertiser 14th September 1839, 1841 census HO107 piece 973 folio 5A/45 page 17, 1851 HO107 piece 2016 folio 360 page 6e, 1861 census piece 1981 Folio 25 Page 3, Staffordshire Gazette and County Standard 30th December 1841, Morning Post 14th March 1842, Ordnance Survey Map 1884

92. Staffordshire Advertiser 4th June 1831, Whites Directory 1834, Staffordshire Advertiser 16th January 1847, The Era 15th September 1850, Nottinghamshire Guardian 6th December 1849, The Era 17 August 1856, The Era 15th September 1850, Whites Directory 1851, London Gazette 6th July 1878, Birmingham Daily Post 6th February 1882, Birmingham Daily Post 4th March 1882, Birmingham Daily Post 31st March 1887, 1891 census Piece: 2218 Folio: 80 Page: 8, Birmingham Daily Post 1st November 1889, 1901 census RG13 piece 2661 folio 72 page 16, 1911 census RG14PN16929 RG78PN1046 RD368 SD1 ED15 SN30, Wolverhampton Red Book 1914

93. Staffordshire Sentinel and Commercial & General Advertiser 24th March 1860, Birmingham Daily Post 8th March 1860, 1861 census RG09 piece 1981 folio 9 page 12, 1871 census RG10 piece 2923 folio 14 page 9, Lichfield Mercury 11th January 1889, Kelly's Directory of Staffordshire 1896, Birmingham Post 13th July 1889

94. Whites Directory 1834, Worcester Journal 17th March 1855, Worcestershire Chronicle 14th March 1855, Birmingham Daily Post 30th June 1859, Wolverhampton Chronicle 6th July 1859, Harrison, Harrod Directory and Gazetteer of Staffordshire 1861, Lichfield Mercury 9th November 1883, Lichfield Mercury 11th January 1889, 1891 census RG12 piece 2218 folio 51 page 5, Preston Chronicle 31st December 1892, Kelly's Directory of Staffordshire 1896, Memoirs of Victor Francis

95. Northampton Mercury 18th December 1819, Stamford Mercury 3rd December 1830, The poll for two knights of the shire to represent the western division of the county of Stafford (1868) by E. Fernie, Kellys Directory, Northampton Mercury 18 December 1886, Lichfield Mercury 8th September 1899, Lichfield Mercury 2nd July 1920, The History of the Kirk Family by Nora M Kirk

96. Staffordshire Advertiser 6th November 1830, Piggots Directory 1834, Whites Directory 1834, Lichfield Mercury 9th November 1883, Lichfield Mercury 15th February 1884, Lichfield Mercury 23rd September 1892, Birmingham Daily Post 8th April 1893, Birmingham Daily Post 10th October 1884, London Gazette Issue 25410 31st October 1884, Lichfield Mercury 5th July 1895, Kellys Directory 1895, Lichfield Mercury 6th February 1914

97. Whites Directory 1834, Tithe Map, 1851 census HO107 piece 2016 folio 343 page 3, Tamworth Herald 16th October 1880, Registry of Deaths Dec 1880 72 Cannock 6b 287, Lichfield Mercury 22nd October 1880, Lichfield Mercury 1st November 1889, Lichfield Mercury 9th February 1900, Lichfield Mercury 18th April 1913

Index

Adams
    Maria, 237
    William, 195
Adie
    John, 211
Albrighton Hunt, 231, 239
Amateur Dramatics, 179
Arden
    John, 181
Aspley Cottage, 88
Aspley Farm, 87, 120, 128, 237
Aston
    James, 69, 169
    Walter, 139, 219
Atkins
    Thomas, 91
Austin
    John Shenstone, 71
Austins
    Charlotte, 190
Avenue Bridge, 141

Badger
    John, 169
Bagatelle, 227
Bailey
    Emily, 196
Baker
    William, 228

Bakery, 223
Ball Lane, 69, 136, 219
Barr Farm, 86
Barrett
    William John, 41
Bassett
    William, 79
Batchelor, 79
Bate
    Phoebe, 206
    Thomas, 79
Beddard
    Arthur, 203
Beech
    Edward, 51
Beeches
    The, 45
Beeches, The, 49, 161, 164
Beer-houses, 223
Bethell
    John, 190
Bickford, 35, 47, 61
    Frank, 47
    George, 189
    Henry, 83, 208
    William, 83, 86, 186, 240
Bickley
    Martha, 223

Biddle
　Henry, 181
Birchcroft, 122
Bird
　Charles, 212
Bishton
　William, 91
Bluebell Cottage, 50
Blyth
　William, 181
Bowdler
　Richard, 122
Bowen
　Arthur, 34
Bowes
　Simpson, 239
Bowling, 228, 239
Brew
　Thomas, 187
Brewery, 192
Brewood & Wolverhampton Railway Company, 116
Brewood Park Cottages, 89
Brewood Park Farm, 41, 52, 53, 89, 141, 144, 145, 204, 231
Brewood Road, 26, 32, 35, 37, 41, 43, 45, 49, 50, 52, 54, 135, 141, 144, 158, 171
Brewood Upper Forge, 54, 145
Bridge Farm, 87
Brinsford, 69
　John, 181
Brinsford Farm, 87
Brinsford Lane, 86
Broad Acres, 26

Broadbent
　Frederick, 205
Bront, The, 145, 147
Brook Cottage, 58
Brook Cottages, 95
Brook House, 41, 54
Brooke
　Richard, 69
Brooke, Edward Adveno, 166
Brookes
　John, 222, 224
Brough
　Elizabeth, 211
Brown
　Joshua, 35
　William, 47
Bryan
　Thomas, 47
　William, 196
Buckley
　Thomas, 236
　William, 236

Cadwallader
　Pauline M, 197
Canals
　Shropshire Union, 89, 116, 141
　Staffs & Worcs, 120, 127, 134, 195, 196, 216, 239
Carbon Works, 115
Careless
　Thomas, 51
Carless
　Littleton, 177
Carter
　George, 200

Cartmail
 Ruth, 208
Cartwright
 John Walker, 237
Cattle Plague, 186
Challinor
 Phoebe, 223
Chambers
 Thomas, 222
Chambley
 Brooke, 163, 190
 Manoah, 163
 Sarah, 165
 William, 47, 81, 163, 190
Chambley Green, 123, 165
Church Alley, 72, 157
Church Lane, 83, 135, 158
Churches and Chapels
 Coven Heath Chapel, 32
 Coven Methodist, 30, 37, 167
 St Paul's, 22, 27, 28, 52, 71, 163, 192, 227
 Sunday School, 30
Cinder Hill, 43, 205
Claygate Road, 69
Clewley, 57
Clifft, 76
 Ann, 225
 Thomas, 157
 William, 69
Coal Mining, 174, 235
Cockett
 John, 181
Coleclough
 Adeline, 192
 Frederick, 37

Coley
 Charles, 73
Cooper
 Joseph, 30, 79
Cope
 Alice, 241
Copeland, 125
Coven Farm, 72
Coven Furnace, 151
Coven Heath Wood, 76, 87, 141
Coven House, 37, 171, 210
Coven Stores, 37
Cowern, 72
Cowley
 George, 112, 187
 Walter, 181
Cowper
 Hugh, 181
Cox
 William, 63
Crateford, 114
Crateford Lane, 69, 121
Cricket, 165
Croft Cottage, 47
Croft, The, 46, 163
Cross Green, 41, 77, 83

Darelyn, 34, 35
Dark Lane, 121, 136, 169
Davies
 Edward, 185
 George, 92
Davis
 Alfred, 204
Daw
 Samuel, 220

Day
　　Felix, 75
Day's Farm, 69
Deakin, 61
Deepmore Mill, 70
Dinosaurs, 52
Dobson, 79
Duncomb, 45
Durham
　　John, 239
Dutton
　　Richard, 181

Earthquake, 206
East Beeches, 45
Emery Mill, 69
Evans
　　William, 112

Farmer
　　Joseph, 50
Faulkner
　　George, 201
Field Names, 96
Fifth Ash, 230
Fisher
　　Crowther Smith, 52
　　Sarah, 52
Floyd
　　Agnes, 181
Foot & Mouth Disease, 186
Forge Cottage, 53
Forrester
　　Reverend, 27
Four Ashes, 50, 71, 96, 113
Four Ashes Farm, 122, 231

Four Ashes Road, 124
Four Ashes Station, 34, 105, 111, 113, 114, 173, 175, 197
Fowler
　　Augustus, 112
　　Sarah, 58
Fox
　　Agnes Maud, 111
Francis
　　Victor, 34

Gallimore
　　Thomas, 198
Gamble
　　John, 209
Gamekeeper, 187, 196, 229
Gawn
　　Douglas, 27
Genner
　　Albert richard, 207
　　Sarah Ann, 208
Giffard, 89
Glover
　　James, 217
Go Plant, 37
Golf Course, 75
Goodacres, 55
Grainger
　　Thomas, 190
Grand Junction Railway, 105, 217
Grange Farm, 41, 43, 54, 63, 76, 125, 157, 225, 229
Green Acres, 126
Green Ivy House, 43
Greenacres, 26
Gregory

Richard, 61
Gregory's Green, 61
Greystones Cottage, 37
Gripton
    William, 79

Hadderley
    John, 224
Haden
    James, 216
Hadley
    John, 43
Hall
    John Handel, 22
    Thomas, 161
Hammersley
    Thomas, 239
Handley
    Bill, 50
Harding
    Frank Henry, 222
Hartshorn, 47
    William, 240
Hayward
    Herbert, 189
    Mary, 158
Heath
    William, 110
Heath House, 55
Hemmingsley
    Mary, 211
Hickman
    Frederick, 193
Higgs
    John, 47
    John Birch, 167

Hill
    Frederick, 61
    Thomas, 223
Hinckes
    Theodosia, 32
Hinks
    Joseph, 209
Hodges
    Edward, 22, 160
Hodgkins
    William, 237
Hollis
    Walter, 41
Holloway
    H E, 222
Holmes, 87
Homage, The, 39, 43, 201
Hood
    Florence, 204
Hordern Cottages, 136
Horse Racing, 164
Hudson
    Henry, 222
Hughes, 46, 47
    Dorothy, 37
    James, 37, 223
    John, 22
    William, 224
Humpage
    Richard, 220

Illedge, 76
    Andrew, 181
Infanticide, 195
Iron Room, 28, 33
Island Pool, 144

Ivy Cottage, 43

Jackson
    Edward, 47
    Joseph, 191, 227
    Joseph Hand, 22
    William, 169
Jackson's Bridge (King's Bridge), 95, 148
James
    Joseph, 47
    Thomas, 211
Jeaven
    Richard, 181
John Smith, 73
Johnson
    Dr Samuel, 52
Jones
    James, 202
    Thomas, 189

K Transport, 63
Keeling
    Frederick J, 91, 187
    Miss, 30
    Robert, 204
Kench
    Charles, 81
Kirk
    Annie Elizabeth, 197
    David, 229
    Edwin, 122, 231
    Samuel Martin, 231
    Sidney, 92, 231
    Stephen, 62, 73, 194

Laches Lane, 145

Laches, The, 26, 69, 83, 120, 165, 198, 227, 237
Latham
    Robert, 239
Lawn Farm, 77, 94, 125, 160, 165
Lawn Lane, 32, 37, 43, 77, 124, 143, 171
Leek
    Edward, 216
Legge
    Lady Joan Margaret, 75
Leverton
    Thomas, 191
Light Ash, 22, 35, 43, 63, 72, 73, 94
Lloyd
    Joseph, 41
Lock-making, 49, 63, 69, 162, 169
Lovatt
    Michael, 88, 206
    Richard, 86
Lower Avenue, 145
Lower Green, 61, 92, 134, 205, 207

Macdonald
    Albert, 112
    Reverend, 30
Mail Coaches, 229, 236
Mannington
    Sarah, 194
Manor Farm, 83
Mansell
    Thomas, 41
    William, 39
Matthews

Alfred, 134
John, 51
McLean, 37
Meadow House, 34
Memorial Hall, 28, 33, 81
Middle Lane, 57
Midland Tar Distillers, 115
Milligan
    James, 224
Monckton, 35, 71
    Edward, 229
    Francis, 205
    Hon. Edward, 124
    Inglis, 27
Moon
    Richard, 79
Morrison
    David, 96
    John, 187
Moseley
    Joseph, 219
Mount Pleasant Farm, 35, 96

Nechells, 55
New Homage Cottages, 43
New Road, 118
Nicholls
    Henry, 202
Nickolds
    Henry, 41
    Titus, 72
Nurseries, The, 39

Oaklands Cottage, 47, 83
Oakley
    Daniel, 222

    Richard, 165, 198, 227, 237
Oginton
    Simon, 69
Old Heath House, 56
Old Mill, 57, 124, 145
Old School House, The, 160
Olerenshaw
    Charles, 96
Orchard Close, 37
Ostler, 159, 220
Owen
    John Frederick, 187

Pacey
    Charles, 207
Paddy
    Andrew, 121
Paddys Lane, 121
Paradise Farm, 83
Paradise Lane, 86, 87, 120
Parkes
    George John, 73
Parson's Croft, 171
Peake
    Fred, 207
Pearson
    William, 236
Pedestrianism, 219
Pendeford Cottage, 58, 144
Pendeford Hall, 57, 143
Pendeford Mill, 141
Penkridge Workhouse, 165
Penkside, 96, 122
Perkin
    James, 88
Piggott

William, 41
Pinfold Lane, 157
Pinke
 Thomas, 181
Piper
 Cyril, 39
Pitchford
 Eleanor, 41
Plant
 Joseph, 201
Poaching, 187
Police Officers
 Barnett, 201
 Bond, 200
 Boyer, 192, 207
 Burton, 191
 Fletcher, 191
 Horn, 237
 Hurmston, 191
 Lawson, 191
 Lawton, 237
 Maguire, 211
 McCabe, 190
 Poulton, 200, 201, 241
 Price, 190
 Snead, 201, 207
 Spendlove, 190
 Titterton, 227
Police Station, 41, 51
Poplars Farm, 45, 49, 81, 159
Poplars Farm Way, 122, 147
Possessions, 182
Post Office, 41, 43
Poultney
 James, 192
Powell
 George, 208
Preston
 James, 34, 35
Price
 William, 69
Public Houses
 Anchor Inn, 35, 44, 50, 83, 124, 135, 192, 193, 200, 239
 Ball Inn, 56, 219
 Black Lion, 88, 216
 Four Ashes Inn, 89, 122, 196, 197, 201, 209, 229
 Harrow Inn, 44, 63, 83, 96, 150, 192, 200, 201, 236
 New Inn, 34, 159, 222, 225
 Rainbow Inn, 43, 49, 158, 200, 201, 223
Pugilism, 209
Pullen
 Clara, 71
 John, 191
 Richard, 71
 Richard Standeford, 71

Railway Accidents, 110
Railway House, 88
Reynolds
 Leonard, 41
 Michael, 175
 Samuel, 91
Richards, 35
 Henry, 41, 45, 47, 83, 182
Rigby
 John, 111
River Penk, 53, 79, 95, 116, 134,

    143
Robb
    James Davidson, 221
Roberts
    Emily, 196
    James, 41
Robinson
    John, 107
    Joseph, 79
Rock Bank (Rat Bank), 195, 202
Rodhouse
    Tom, 228
Rolliston
    Richard, 56
Rookery, The, 43, 59, 134
Rope-making, 216
Roper
    Reverend G, 27
Rowlands
    George, 27
Royal Ordnance Factory, 83, 118, 125

Saredon Brook, 70, 116, 134, 150, 152, 239
Scattergood
    Edwin, 241
School, 22
School Lane, 26, 44, 45, 54, 60
Schoolbred
    William, 57
Sewage Works, 70
    Coven, 134
    Coven Heath, 134
Shadow Factory, 93
Shaw Hall, 125
Shaw Hall Lane, 69
Shaw Lane, 125
Shemilt
    William, 237
Shenstone, 35, 37, 60
    William, 70
Sherrett
    Henry, 46
Shooting, 92, 163, 219, 237
Shotton
    Samuel and Thomas, 43
Simms
    Joe, 73
    William, 63
Simpson, 86
Slade Heath Railway Bridge, 109
Slater
    Henry, 87
    Richard, 69
Slaughterhouse, 228
Smith
    Charles, 75
    George, 37
    John, 30, 45, 47, 49, 95, 167, 224
    Joseph, 91, 92
Somerford Hall, 52
Somerford Lane, 52
Somerford Wood, 124
Spicer
    Emma, 225
Spilsbury
    Thomas, 219
Spinke
    Thomas, 181
Spring, 145

Spruce
   Richard, 209
Stafford Road, 50, 60, 63, 73, 96, 120, 123, 124, 139, 197, 216, 236
Standeford Bridge, 79, 151, 236
Standeford Cottage, 62, 71, 166
Standeford Farm, 124
Standeford Green, 44, 134
Standeford Lodge, 27, 62
Standeford Mill, 37, 43, 63, 70, 72, 150, 191
Star Mobile Home Park, 65
Station Drive, 236
Steam Engines, 126, 129, 167, 170, 173
Steene
   Jane, 181
Stone House, 52
Stradsfield Quarry, 52, 91
Surnames, 179

Tarmac, 37
Taylor
   Kate, 200
Telephone Exchange, 33
Terry
   William, 181
Thacker
   Roseanna, 228
Thompson
   Ann, 56
   George, 237
Thorneycroft
   Edward, 56
Three Hammers Farm, 73, 134

Till
   Frank, 34
   Philip, 35
   William, 46
Tomkys
   Joseph, 227
Towers
   Henry, 56
Townsend
   Joseph, 50
Tranter
   Benjamin, 221
   Edwin, 239
Tunckes
   Richard, 181
Turner
   Arthur, 94
Turnpikes, 229
Typhoid, 186

Vaughan
   Elizabeth, 223
   George, 210
Venables
   George W, 222
Vicarage, The, 160
Village Foundry, 37, 171, 177

Wade
   Charles, 88
   Thomas, 34
Walhouse
   William, 89
Walker
   Alfred, 241
War Memorial, 81

Ward
  Alfred, 201, 204
  Edwin, 194
  Jane, 229
  Joseph, 209, 229
  Samuel, 229
  Sarah Elizabeth, 205
Waring
  Richard, 202
  William, 237
Warrington
  Basil, 89
Wassall
  Winifred, 34
Water Pumping Stations
  Slade Heath, 127
  Somerford, 127
Water Pumps, 129
Watershead Brook, 79, 145, 159
Watkins
  Thomas, 91
Wayside Cottage, 63
Wedge
  Michael, 71
Weekes
  William, 181
Wells
  Joseph, 227
West Beeches, 45
Whalley
  Dick, 75
Whatton
  Arthur, 43, 60
Wheelwright, 50, 220
White
  Charles, 92

White Lodge, 62
Wiggin
  Henry, 34
Wiggins Stores, 34, 223
Williams
  Catherine, 41
  John, 22
  Jonathon, 50
  Thomas, 50
Willington
  Edward, 56, 57, 75
Willmer
  John, 192
Wilson
  Joseph, 91
Windmill, 69
Woodlands, The, 61, 92
Wootton
  Jonah, 88
  Joseph G, 190
Wright
  Ann, 223

Yates
  James, 223
  Joseph, 75
Yeomans, 71
  Annie Elizabeth, 231
  John, 212
  Moses, 96

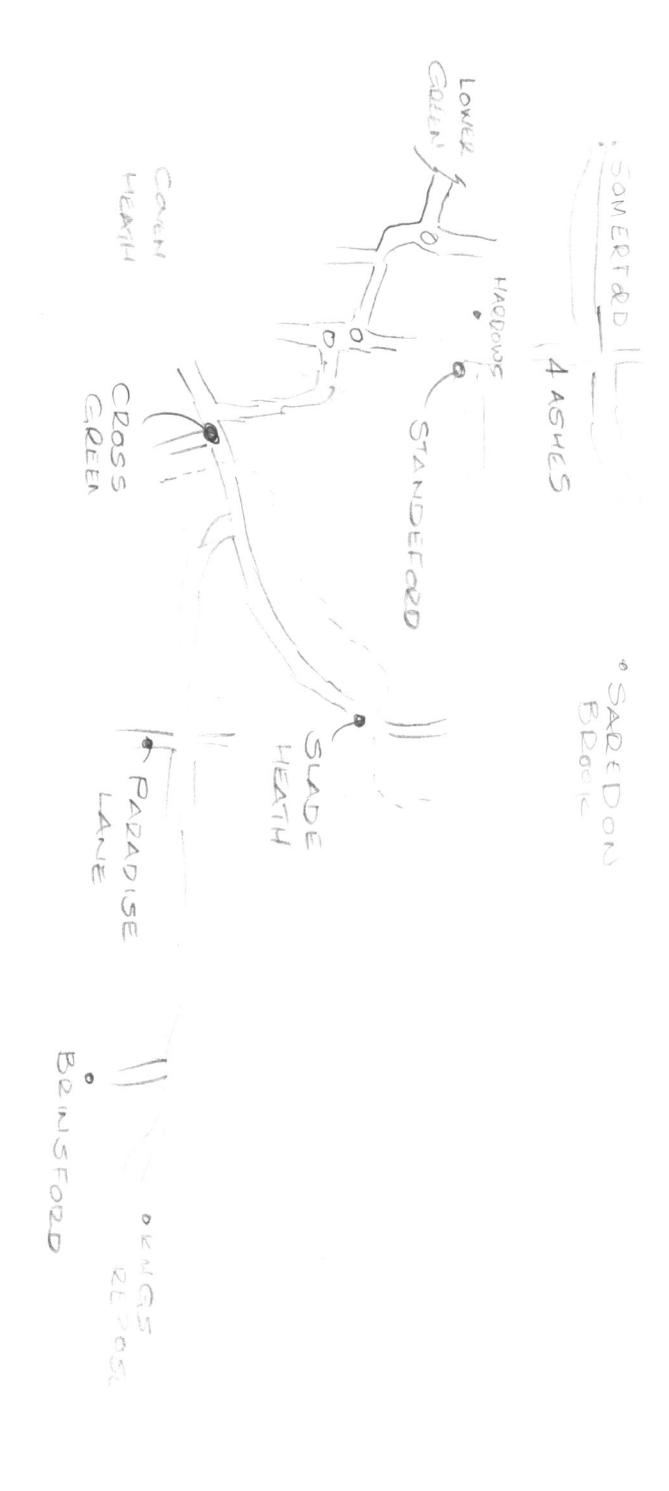